The Abolition Movement
An Anthology

The Abolition Movement
An Anthology

Edited with an Introduction by
Stephanie L. Harrington

WHITLOCK PUBLISHING
Alfred, New York

First Whitlock Publishing edition 2015

Whitlock Publishing
P.O. Box 472
Alfred, NY 14802

Editorial matter © Stephanie L. Harrington

ISBN 13: 978-1-943115-08-2

This book was set in Adobe Garamond Pro on 55# acid-free paper that meets ANSI standards for archival quality.

Printed in the United States of America.

Contents

Introduction   i

Chronology of the Transatlantic Slave Trade   xi

Bibliography   xiii

Note on the Text   xiv

Primary Documents

Brief Considerations on Slavery   1

To the Friends of the Abolition of the Slave Trade   13

A Letter on the Greater Necessity of an Abolition of the African Slave Trade   18

Hints for a Specific Plan for an Abolition of the Slave Trade   30

Slave Narrative

Thoughts and Sentiments by Ottobah Cugoano   51

Poetry

Poems by William Cowper   148

Poems by Robert Southey   156

Suggested Reading   167

INTRODUCTION

"But yet, admit the Sire his Right foregoes,
Can he his Childrens sep'rate Claim dispose?
Whate'er the Parent gave; whate'er he give;
They who have Right to Life, have Right to live:
And Spight of Man's Consent, or Man's Decree,
A Right to Life, is Right to Liberty."

Anon: Epistle to Lord Cornbury.

FOR CENTURIES, hundreds of thousands of African men,
women and children were denied their basic liberties as they
were subjected to the slave trade, forever changing their lives
and the ways of the world. After being ripped from their homes, they
were placed on ships as cargo to be distributed around the world to
the highest bidder, treated like nothing more than breathing pieces
of property.

From the sixteenth to nineteenth centuries, the cruel treatment
of these men and women rarely questioned except by the abolitionists. The abolition movement in England came to attention in the late
1700s, beginning with the lobbying against the slave trade and the ruling of the Somerset case in 1772. Despite these small steps, the majority of the population had little interest in ending the human trafficking

to which they had become so accustomed. England continued to ship enslaved Africans around the world to be sold.

This anthology brings to life the reality of England's transatlantic slave trade and the movement to end its practice. Published here are four abolitionist essays, anti-slavery poems by William Cowper and Robert Southey, and *Thoughts and Sentiments on the Evil of Slavery*, a slave narrative by Ottobah Cugoano.

The Beginnings of English Involvement in the Slave Trade

English relations with Africans predated the transatlantic slave trade by at least one hundred years, focusing primarily on the exchange of English metal, woolens, beads, gun powder, and firearms for African gold, ivory, and wax. While other European nations such as France, Spain, and the Netherlands found profit through the buying and selling of men, women and children who were forcefully taken from West Africa to supply forced labor, merchants in England at first avoided this practice. This changed in the mid sixteenth century, however, when England finally succumbed to the seemingly cheap labor that the slave trade offered. Despite this delayed entrance into the transatlantic slave trade, the strength of the national government and a large merchant class quickly made England one of the leading carriers of enslaved Africans.

The first English voyages to West Africa with the intentions of returning with slaves were conducted by John Hawkins between 1562 and 1567. During his first two voyages, Hawkins led Englishmen to the coast of West Africa, returning with three hundred to four hundred slaves per trip. A third voyage set sail in 1567, partially endorsed by Queen Elizabeth I, and concluded with Hawkins participating in a local war, helping one African ruler fight against another. His actions resulted in a payment of Africans, adding his total of collected slaves to approximately 1,200 men and women, though he lost nearly everything from this final voyage during the return to England due to a storm. After Hawkins' final voyage, England's participation in the trade declined and instead a more traditional commerce of goods and materials was encouraged by the ruling party.

England lay dormant in regards to the slave trade for nearly a hundred years, until the establishment of the Guinea Company in 1651, resurrecting the desire for African labor and the intentions of once again trafficking slaves from Western Africa. Over the next several years, the slave trade was expanded both by private traders and businesses such as the Company of Royal Adventurers and the Royal African Company. The later companies were endorsed by a combination of royal and wealthy figures, merchants and cavaliers, and subscribers and shareholders who wanted a personal investment in the profits of the growing commerce of Africans.

Sources and Destinations

At the beginning of the rise of their involvement in the transatlantic slave trade in the 1700s, the English were exporting somewhere in the range of nine thousand slaves per year, primarily from the west coast of Africa to their various territories. This number increased astronomically throughout the century, reaching nearly 45,000 slaves exported each year. With the increased demand for slave labor, English traders began to expand their stations where slaves were obtained, focusing primarily on six regions: the Gold Coast, the Northern Parts of Guinea, the Windward Coast (also called the Sierra Leone region), Andra and Whydah, Benin and the Calabar Rivers, and Angola.

Hundreds of ships brought English merchants, with the highest percentage departing from Liverpool, to these ports to conduct two types of trade: shore trade and ship trade. Shore trade focused on exchanges within the forts and factories at the Northern Parts of Guinea and the Gold Coast, but it was the less popular of the two types of trade due to the inflexibility of market locations. Ship trade proved to be more profitable, in turn making it the preferred method of trading. Merchants preferred to hire ships to make the voyage from England to Africa where they would gather slaves and then depart for the West Indies where their new cargo was sold. At this time, the transatlantic trade did not follow the triangular route with which it is so often associated. At the beginning of the trade, it was not profitable for merchants to have the ships return from the West Indies to England with products, so this final side of the triangle was not put into place until much later, when a significant profit could be made from selling these goods.

Once upon the slaving ships, the enslaved were destined for one of the British colonies in the West Indies, though during the late 17th century one in four Africans were lost during travels due to poor conditions on the ships, malnutrition, and maltreatment at the hands of the captain and the crew. The destinations for these ships included Antigua, Jamaica, Monterrat and other small islands where cheap labor was highly valued. The most frequented port for the slave trade was Barbados, a British island in the Caribbean that was known as "the brightest jewel in His Majesty's crown" due to the fact that it was the highest producer of sugar, England's most profitable import.

Prices and Profits

Prices of slaves and overall profits of the trade are some of the hardest facts and figures of the trade to confirm, though even in the early years the worth was calculated to be anywhere between £200,000 and £300,000 per year. The large range is a result of varying prices from one region to another, as well as differences within that region. Supply and demand was the leading factor that influenced the pricing of slaves, sometimes due to pressure from war or competition with other regions or ports as well as illegal slave traders, though it is believed that each slave is estimated to have cost approximately £50.

Despite the difficulty of collecting information in this field, it has been noted that the highest prices were found in Gamba and Angola, while the lowest were recorded in Whydahs. Overall, however, the most profitable regions during the transatlantic slave trade were the Senegambia and Sierra Leone regions.

The Abolition Movement

In *The Anti-Slavery Movement in England*, author Frank J. Klingerberg states that:

> The century after the peace of Utrecht can be divided into two parts; the first fifty years are characterized by stray voices raised in opposition but without any effective steps against either the slave trade or slavery. The second half of the century is characterized by active, organized opposition leading to emancipation in England in 1772 [. . .], to the destruction of the trade in 1806 and 1807, and to the attempts to secure universal abolition at the congress of Vienna.[*]

The abolition movement started with whispers questioning the commerce of slaves in the early eighteenth century, questions that were beginning to address the treatment of enslaved men and women, the markets in which they were sold, and the institution that supported the continuation of the trade.

These whispers first began amongst the Quakers and their founder, George Fox, as early as 1671, but measures against members who endorsed the slave trade were not made until nearly a century later. The first individual to directly challenge the institution supporting the slave trade was English civil servant Granville Sharp. Sharp aided various political cases during his career, but did not become notably interested in the abolition movement until 1767. While working in the ordnance department, he discovered the case of Jonathan Strong, an

[*] Frank J. Klingberg, *The Anti-Slavery Movement in England* (Archon Books, 1963), 22-23.

enslaved African man who Sharp helped return to full health after the man was beaten and then discarded by his master. Sharp's actions were then scrutinized by Strong's previous master and the courts who were questioning his recovery of the slave, an event that sparked the flame that would be Granville Sharp's future as an abolitionist. In the following years, Sharp began to write and distribute pamphlets containing the laws of England, the opinions of the Lord Chief Justice, and his own argument against the laws that would forcefully return a slave to his or her owner. These pamphlets were distributed to various lawyers in an attempt to make a difference when such cases were brought before the court. His efforts appeared futile, that is until the case of James Somerset was brought to attention in 1772. Somerset's emancipation was delayed through multiple court terms, seemingly due to the unwillingness of the judge to emancipate all other enslaved Africans that this verdict would also apply to, an emancipation that would free between 14,000 and 15,000 slaves and result in the equivalence of a loss of £700,000 worth of laboring property. Ultimately Somerset was freed, in turn abolishing slavery in the British Isles, a decision that set precedents for monarchs in other nations regarding the acceptance of the slave trade. The efforts of Granville Sharp in the Somerset case caused a considerable push towards abolition, but was still only the first step in the long journey that was to come.

Granville Sharp and others abolitionists like him were followed by a new group of humanitarians, a group that "did not exhaust themselves in religious strife; rather, they devoted their lives and fortunes to the remedying of practical evils."[*] Of this new wave of abolitionists, the most well known was William Wilberforce, a man who publicized his opinions and principles in works such as his 1797 *A Practical View of the Prevailing Religious System of Professed Christians*. Wilberforce started his political career by entering parliament in Hull in 1780, the

[*] Frank J. Klingberg, *The Anti-Slavery Movement in England* (Archon Books, 1963), 25.

same city in which he was born twenty-one years earlier. After participating in a trip to Nice four years later, Wilberforce became interested in religious introspection, believing that it was the responsibility of a Christian to lead the way in movements and reforms that were morally necessary. One reformation that he applied this belief to is that of the slave trade: his investigation into the practice grew quickly as he sought information from merchants who participated in the slave trade and discussed the issue of slavery with other interested men. Despite this growing focus on the slave trade, Wilberforce never officially joined the committee of abolitionists. Instead, he decided to work closely with its members to help put a stop to the trafficking of Africans and is credited with bringing many proposals and legislations before the court in an attempt to abolish the enslavement of men, women and children throughout England and her territories.

During the centuries that the slave trade was practiced, many types of abolitionists made their voices heard. Granville Sharp and William Wilberforce are two of the big names of the movement, and they are the men who are credited with initiating action, pursuing reformation, and demanding abolition of the enslaved Africans throughout European nations and their territories. There are, however, still other types of abolitionists including first-hand advocates, the men with primary knowledge concerning the trade, how plantations operate, and the life of the slave on these plantations. Men who fit this description include James Ramsay, James Stephen and Zachary Macaulay. Activists such as these men were invaluable to the humanitarian movement that was occurring, for they were able to provide personal information focused on direct involvement in the trade, information that had the power to intrigue and disturb any audience who was willing to listen, information that could help promote the abolition movement.

Another type of activist for abolition came at various points throughout the movement: abolitionist writers. These are the men and women who wrote pamphlets and letters advocating for the rights of

Africans as well as the poets and novelists who wrote literature that drew attention to human trafficking. Another form of literature that sheds light upon the trafficking of Africans is the slave narrative, a personal recollection of a man or woman who was a victim of the slave trade. One such work is published in this collection: *Thoughts and Sentiments on the Evil and Wicked Traffic of the Slavery and Commerce of the Human Species* by Ottobah Cugoano.

The effectiveness of the abolition movement depended not on the medium that was used to relay information, as can be seen through these many approaches, but on the perseverance and desire to make a difference demonstrated bu these advocates. The road to total abolition was not an easy one: pamphlets were printed and distributed, many bills were proposed and denied, and a countless number of Africans were forcefully removed from their homes to work away their lives on plantations. The efforts of English abolitionists were finally rewarded in 1833 when a legislation proposing the total abolition of slavery was passed.

Opposition to Abolition

Many Europeans supported the transatlantic slave trade throughout its most popular days, believing that:

> the trade was necessary to the further development of the West Indies, upon which the security of Britain, the strength of its navy, and the permanence of its manufacturers so greatly depended; that agriculture could not be carried on there without slaves; that the trade had been guaranteed and even encouraged by a large number of acts of parliament, on the faith of which many men had invested their fortunes in the islands; that even if Great Britain abolished the trade, it would be vigorously carried on by her rivals, who eagerly sought it; that the trade, instead of being abolished, ought to receive the encouragement of parliament in the face of fierce

foreign competition; and finally, that the propositions were unjust because they would take away private property without compensation.*

Many people in England objected the abolition of the slave trade for one reason or another, and many of those reasons are outlined by Klingberg in the above quote. Like the abolitionists, many of the anti-abolitionists published their opinions and practices in various forms to be distributed to the public. One example of this type of publication is *Doubts on the Abolition of the Slave Trade*, a doctrine that was written by an older member of parliament that captures the beliefs of those who opposed the slave trade.

Some of the points that are made in this document are doubts on the impiety, injustice, and inhumanity in regards to the slave trade, the necessity of the cheap labor that slavery offers to cultivate the plantations that fund life in the mother countries, and general objections to abolition. The ultimate goal of works such as these was to convince both the general public and lawmakers that the astronomical number of slaves taken from the various regions and ports throughout Africa was, in fact, necessary to the survival of the current state of living in England.

Immediate and Lasting Effects of the Transatlantic Slave Trade

During the height of the transatlantic slave trade, many believed that the merchants, farmers, and consumers were so dependent upon human trafficking that the life of the English would fall apart at the seams without the practice. While there was a conceived necessity for enslaved Africans throughout European territories to work on and cultivate the fields that supplied the mother countries with the goods they so eagerly consumed, such as sugar and tobacco, the transportation via ship that is so famously associated with the trade was costly, and

* Frank J. Klingberg, *The Anti-Slavery Movement in England* (Archon Books, 1963), 85-86.

expenses were raised for merchants who owned their ships rather than hiring an individual ship or fleet. Despite the costs, both financially and in the lives of slaves, the trade brought about a shift in trading practices from an organized monopoly to free trade in the hands of merchants.

Although slavery was abolished in England nearly 200 years ago, our contemporary world is far from free of the shadow of the practice. Understanding social inequality, racism, and cultural attitudes today requires an understanding of slavery's disturbing history. Modern audiences are familiarized with the practices of the slave trade predominantly through films such as *Amazing Grace* (2006), *Lincoln* (2012), *Twelve Years a Slave* (a memoir published in 1853 turned film in 2013), and *Belle* (2013). Other reminders of the evils of slavery include informational texts and novels, music, and laws regarding affirmative action.

This volume of abolitionist texts brings to light some of the important voices that originally spoke against slavery. It represents one piece in the effort to ensure that the hundreds of thousands of Africans who were forcefully taken from their homes and enslaved throughout European nations and territories will not be forgotten any time soon. The republication of the information in this anthology works to preserve the history of a tumultuous time in England's past, and by keeping that history alive, ideally help protect the basic liberties of every man, woman, and child.

STEPHANIE HARRINGTON

The Slave Trade in England

1555   John Lok, a London merchant, brings a group of Africans to England in order to teach them English so they can act as interpreters in their native land.

1562   Slaves are transported to England for the first time by John Hawkins.

1618   King James I founds The Company of Adventurers of London Trading into the Parts of Africa.

1620s England becomes established in the slave trade.

1672   The Royal African Company, financed by royal, aristocratic, and commercial capital, is formed to regulate the slave trade.

1698   Trade is opened to private traders from Bristol and Liver pool due to the end of the Royal African Company.

1713   The Treaty of Utrecht awards the "Asiento" to Britain, giving them the sole right to import an unlimited number of slaves to the Spanish Caribbean colonies for thirty years.

1760s Granville Sharp begins to lobby against the slave trade.

1772   The Somerset case declares any slave who sets foot in Britain is free.

1773   Brief Considerations on Slavery is published.

1776   David Hartley introduces the first anti-slave legislation to Parliament.

1783   British Quakers form a committee against slave trade.

1787   Thoughts and Sentiments by Ottobah Cugoano is published.

The Society for Effecting the Abolition of the African Slave Trade is founded in London.

1788   William Cowper's poems concerning the slave trade are published.

Hints for a Specific Plan for an Abolition of the Slave Trade is published.

1789   William Blake publishes "The Little Black Boy" in Songs of Experience.

1790   The first bill for the abolition of the slave trade fails.

1791   Wilberforce proposes a bill for the abolition of the slave trade which is defeated by a vote of 163 to 88.

1792   The House of Lords reject an abolition bill passed by the House of Commons.

        A Letter on the Greater Necessity of an Abolition of the African Slave Trade is published.

1794-98 William Southey's sonnets and poems concerning the slave trade are published.

1804   St. Domingue (now Haiti) becomes the first independent black state outside Africa.

1806   Wilberforce's legislation passes and becomes law the following year.

1807   Parliament abolishes slavery in British territories.

1823   Wilberforce and Thomas Fowell Buxton raise the issue of abolishing slavery altogether.

1833   Wilberforce's and Buxton's legislation passes.

1838   Slavery ended in British colonies.

Bibliography

Doubts on the Abolition of the Slave Trade. London, 1790.

Klingberg, Frank J. *The Anti-Slavery Movement in England: A Study in English Humanitarianism.* Archon Books, 1968. Print.

Rawley, James A., and Stephen D. Behrendt. *The Transatlantic Slave Trade : A History.* Lincoln: University of Nebraska Press, 2005. *eBook Collection (EBSCOhost).* Web.

Thomas, Hugh. *The Slave Trade: the Story of the Atlantic Slave Trade, 1440-1870.* New York: Simon & Schuster, 1997.

Note on the Text

The pieces found within this anthology are based on eighteenth century editions. Archaic spellings and phrasings were preserved in order to maintain the authenticity of the literature.

The Abolition Movement
An Anthology

Brief Considerations on Slavery, and the Expediency of its Abolition

Brief Considerations on Slavery, and the Expediency of its Abolition.

With some Hints on the Means whereby it may be gradually effected.

Recommended to the serious Attention of all, and especially of those entrusted with the Powers of Legislation.

But yet, admit the Sire his Right foregoes,
Can he his Childrens sep'rate Claim dispose?
Whate'er the Parent gave; whate'er he give;
They who have Right to Life, have Right to live;
And Spight of Man's Consent, or Man's Decree,
A Right to Life, is Right to Liberty.

Anon: Epistle to Lord Cornbury.

BURLINGTON:
Printed and Sold by ISAAC COLLINS,
M.DCC.LXXIII.
BRIEF CONSIDERATIONS ON SLAVERY, &c.

Brief Considerations on Slavery, &c.

The religious and moral Obligations we are under in a private capacity, to do our utmost to promote the true interests of mankind, encrease with our powers and opportunities of action. Hence arises the importance of that trust, which the wisdom of government has reposed in legislatures; in discharging which, having the will, they have also the power of promoting those interests in the most effectual manner. The object therefore, which I now take the liberty of recommending to their attention, has an indisputable claim to it; not only from its importance as relating to the community, but from a consideration which must give it great additional weight with every generous mind—the incapacity of those on whose behalf it is solicited, to plead their own cause. It is the case of the enslaved Africans—a case which tho' familiarized to us by custom, is yet in all its parts so replete with affecting circumstances, that perhaps it has not its parallel in the history of any period of time; and attended with the particular aggravation, of being acted under a government, remarkable above all others for the excellence of its constitution, and the equity of its laws. How it has happened that a nation, which has so eminently distinguished itself in asserting the common rights of mankind, and which has so often generously interposed its power for the relief of its oppressed neighbours, should tolerate so grievous an infringement of liberty in its own dominions, is difficult to comprehend. But my intention is not to expatiate on the inconsistency of these generous exertions of its power, with the toleration of the African slave-trade. I hope it may be attributed to the multiplicity and weight of other engagements, which have so much engrossed the attention of government, that the iniquitous nature of this traffick has not been adverted to; for certainly an acquaintance with it, could only be necessary for its suppression. But without a further investigation of the cause, it is more to my present purpose, to confine myself to such considerations, as being duly attended to, may assist the cure of this malignant disorder in the body politick. With this view, I shall briefly consider its inconsistency with the divine, as well as the social law; its impolicy and evil tendency; and then endeavour to point out the most probable means by which the evil may be remedied.

It cannot be denied that Slavery was allowed to the Israelites by the Mosaic law, under certain circumstances and restrictions; yet it differed from this of the Africans in several important particulars. Their

3

bondmen and bondwomen enjoyed many privileges; and in the year of Jubilee, liberty was proclaimed unto all the inhabitants of the land. On the contrary, a large part of our poor African slaves, have no ground to expect the most distant admission to liberty, for either themselves, or their latest posterity. But even though we may conceive Slavery to be reconcileable to the precepts given under that dispensation; yet to every unprejudiced mind, it must appear totally repugnant to the spirit and design of the gospel, the import of which was announced to the world, in a manner awfully expressive of its superior excellence, proclaiming "Glory to God in the highest; peace on earth; and good will to men." These glorious purposes, our blessed Saviour, when personally among men, inculcated by his example and doctrines; and, to give these greater efficacy, finally sealed them with his blood. Various were the precepts he delivered, but those relating to our social duties, are all comprized in that excellent command, "Therefore whatsoever ye would that men should do to you, do ye even so to them; for this is the law and the prophets." Mat. 7.12. St. Paul's opinion of those concerned in the practice now under consideration, appears by his enumerating them among a number of atrocious offenders for whom the law was made, viz. "Murderers of fathers; murderers of mothers; manslayers; whoremongers; them that defile themselves with mankind; menstealers," &c.

That it is also an offence against the social law, cannot be contradicted; for this law is founded on the necessity of mutual security, and a reciprocation of benefits; and by the light of our natural reason, we cannot find a rule better adapted to promote these ends, than that I have quoted from the vii. of Matthew; to which both Christians and Pagans have joined in giving the distinguishing appellation of the golden rule. The celebrated Montesquieu and many others who have made the rights of mankind their particular study, assert that men universally have an inherent title to Liberty; and the author I have named, with no less strength than vivacity of reasoning, has refuted those ridiculous arguments, which interested men have been obliged to adduce, in support of a pretended opinion, that the colour or unpolished manners of the Africans, can operate against their claim to this first of temporal enjoyments.

In these northern provinces there are not very many, who are immediately concerned in the trade to Africa for Slaves; nor is the number of these oppressed people very considerable, when compared with that of many other colonies. Hence some, though admitting the injustice of the slave trade in general, may yet be unwilling to view it as a matter sufficiently important for the extraordinary interposition of a legislature; being perhaps insensibly biased by interest, the prevalence of custom, or the example of less enlightened times; thus lessening the force of those objections which calm reflection had suggested. I would submit to the consideration of such, the complicated distress these poor creatures suffer, in being forceably torn from that portion of happiness, which the allwise Creator allotted to them in their native state; to sustain for life, a bondage which, in our southern colonies and islands, is more cruel and oppressive than the most of us in the northern colonies have had an opportunity of forming any idea of. Add to this, the bloody wars occasioned by this infernal trade—the great proportion of them who die on the passage to, and in what is called the seasoning in America; and can we then hesitate a moment, in determining on the expediency of contributing whatever lies in our power to discourage it. It is true some of our forefathers, and some of the present generation, may have been, and yet are in the practice of buying and selling slaves. The reasons against it, but a few years ago, were not so well understood as they now are. The opportunities of information are become more frequent; and the usage of them in general among us, has been less likely to excite an inquiry into the nature of the trade, and our title to their services. The practice of ages cannot sanctify error; but the progress of reformation has, in all, been gradual. I doubt not there are now many men in England, whose integrity we should revere, but who, for want of proper information or attention to the subject, do yet admit the right of the British parliament to tax the colonies; but we are not, for that reason obliged to admit it. Having thus briefly considered the slave-trade as contradictory to the divine and social law, it is needless to urge the impropriety of any, and especially a free people being in anywise concerned in it. I shall therefore proceed to consider the particular inconveniences attending it, with respect to the community.

That the trade is attended with many inconveniences of an evil and impolitic tendency, has been lately clearly set forth by several writers. It will be sufficient for me to enumerate a few of them. Every thing that debases the mind, unfits it for society; and this is a distinguishing characteristick of Slavery, which naturally suppresses every generous expansion of the mind. Montesquieu, in his spirit of laws faith, "That nothing more assimilates a man to a beast, than living among freemen, himself a slave: such people as these are the natural enemies of society;

and their number must always be dangerous." Therefore the having slaves in our families or neighbourhood, must have a pernicious effect on the principles and morals of our young people and servants. May we not fear that religion and morality, industry and publick spirit, have nearly declined in proportion as it has been encouraged?—The riches of a free state consists in the number of members, who enjoying its privileges and blessings, are thereby interested in its preservation and advancement. Every slave among us occupies the room of a free person, and not only lessens the riches of the state by diminishing the number of its friends, but adds one to that of its internal enemies; for such every one must be accounted, who can derive no hope from its prosperity, and may possibly be benefited by its ruin.* While on the other hand, every servant on the expiration of a limited servitude, setting out with the animating hope of acquiring an independence in the community, and of enjoying the blessings of life, and the protection of the laws, heartily unites in promoting the prosperity of his country; and, as that hope is answered with success, becomes more and more deeply interested in its safety: the beneficial effects of this on our lands and produce, are very extensive, and too obvious to need a recital.—In the present contest between Great Britain and her colonies, it seems particularly necessary on our parts to convince her, that our opposition to her claims is not merely from selfish motives—not only made because they happen to affect our particular interests; but from a disinterested generous love to liberty, founded on principle—on publick virtue, and a conviction that it is the unalienable right of man. But how can she believe this, when, so loudly complaining of her attacks on our political liberty, all the colonies tolerate, and many of them greatly encourage this violent invasion of natural liberty; subjecting the Africans not only to the deprivation of all property, but even to the most abject state of perpetual personal slavery? If we suppose the divine blessing is necessary to ensure us success in asserting our rights; of how much consequence is it, that we should practise the part enjoined by the divine command, "Whatsoever ye would that men should do to you, do ye even so to them?" If power only must determine our right, how little have we to expect? On the other hand, were we armed with conscious innocence, and supported by the justice of our cause; what have we

* Admitting this, what danger must attend our southern colonies, in some of which, the proportion of slaves to freemen is greater than as twelve to one?

to fear? With what confidence might we urge our claims? But as a late writer on this subject observes, "If we need the help of the negroes; so does Great-Britain need our help to pay off their national debt. If we desire to grow rich, and rest at ease by their toils and labours; so does Great-Britain desire the same at our expence. So that while we persist in this practice of enslaving the Africans, our mouths ought to be entirely shut, as to any duties and taxes which Great-Britain may see cause to lay upon us. Otherwise I see not, but that out of our own mouths, or by our own practice, we may be justly condemned."

Having given my sentiments on a trade and practice, which, to use the words of the author of An essay in vindication of the continental colonies of America, "Policy rejects; justice condemns; and piety dissuades;" I shall, from the same respectable author, add, "Shall Americans persist in a conduct which cannot be justified; or persevere in oppression, from which their hearts must recoil? If the barbarous Africans shall continue to enslave each other; let the daemon slavery remain among them, that their crime may include its punishment. Let not Christians, by administering to their wickedness, confess their religion to be a useless refinement, their profession vain, and themselves as inhuman as the savages they detest."

I cannot believe there are any in the Christian faith, who have attentively, and dispassionately considered the subject, but will adopt the opinion, that Slavery, in any case, cannot be justified—that, as it is conducted in the African trade, it is a most cruel, tyrannical and violent invasion of the sacred rights of mankind; and highly offensive to Almighty God—that it is impolitick in its nature—that the practice of buying and selling slaves among ourselves is an evident encouragement of the trade; and that the encouragement of it, by any means, is inconsistent with our civil and religious interests. If we thus believe, it is certainly our indispensable duty in every station, publick or private, to exert ourselves for its suppression, whatever difficulties may be apprehended to attend its final accomplishment. The prejudices of custom are strong—those imbibed from interest, yet stronger. But in such a cause, we may be assured the blessing of Omnipotence will attend our endeavors, and in due time crown them with success; not within our own limits only; but our example will most probably have a happy influence on the conduct of others more remote. It lies in our power, in some measure, to atone for the wrongs our ancestors or ourselves have inadvertently imposed on these oppressed people in time past.

Is not then the first and most important step, absolutely to prohib-it any future importations into these colonies? If by royal instructions, our governors are prevented the exercise of their own judgments; pro-vincial addresses to the crown, would be likely to remove the difficulty. The sense of the people, conveyed by their representatives to the royal ear, on so interesting a subject, must prevail, with a prince whose vir-tues have endeared him to his people, although it should be opposed by men, comparatively few in number; whose avarice may continue to render them insensible to the common feelings of humanity, and whose GOD is gain. If we cannot obtain a total prohibition of the im-portation, we shall certainly be indulged in obtaining it for the colonies which petition for it. Even should we fail here, the conscious satisfac-tion of having done our duty, will be a reward sufficient for the labour.

With respect to the slaves already among us, the case is more dif-ficult, and will consequently occasion a diversity of sentiments on the proper means of effecting their enlargement. The first question is, what does justice require? This being determined, the honest mind will en-deavour to practise it. There are many of this character, who, in pursu-ing the inquiry, have inclined to an opinion, that some of these unhap-py people are unfit for liberty; and that their manumission would be attended with ruin to themselves. Such a state of depravity is not im-possible, and nothing so likely to occasion it, as a long continuance in the situation they have been in. I wish there may not be many instances of this kind. Where it happens to be the case, and the possessor, after carefully divesting himself of any sinister bias, can justify a detention on this motive, I shall not controvert his right to exercise his judgment. There are also many, who not being yet sufficiently acquainted with the subject, to see the iniquity of the practice, do not apprehend the neces-sity of releasing their slaves. As these would be inclined to oppose, and those I have before mentioned, for other reasons, may be rather averse to a general and indiscriminate manumission; we may perhaps infer the expediency of postponing that desirable work to a period more favourable to our wishes. In reformations of all kinds, where conviction precedes conversion, the effect is most permanent. But no objections occur to me, to the framing such laws, as will leave people at liberty to emancipate their slaves under certain restrictions.

As the laws stand at present in several of our northern govern-ments, the act of manumission is clogged with difficulties that almost amount to a prohibition. An amendment is therefore necessary; and may be effected with advantage to the community. We may suppose all the laws alluded to, are intended to secure the publick from being chargeable with any expence, in case the manumised slave should by age, sickness, or other disability, become incapable of supporting himself: and a provision of this nature seems highly reasonable in certain cases. If, for instance, a slave is become aged and infirm in my service, it is unreasonable I should have it in my power, by manumission to deny him a support from my estate, to which perhaps his labour had contributed. But if, on the other hand, I have received no other benefit from his labour, than what was a proper compensation for the instruction I have given him, and the publick afterwards receives that benefit, it is then as reasonable, that the publick should be chargeable with any expence, occasioned by such disability. This seems to be the general principle on which our laws relating to paupers are formed; and I see no inconvenience in adopting it in the case now under consideration.

Admitting then, that if a slave is set at liberty at the age of twenty-one years, the publick afterwards receives all the benefit of his labour, it will follow that I may set him free at that age, clear of any charge or incumbrance on my estate. If I detain him longer, and then give him his liberty, the same reasoning supposes, that if the publick is afterwards liable to support him, in case of disability, I must pay the publick a certain sum of money proportionable to the time of such detention exceeding twenty-one years. No general rule can be exactly adapted to all cases. But I believe a law formed on these principles, would not only greatly tend to the relief of individuals, but remove some objections, to which I apprehend the present laws of several provinces are liable; particularly those which permit manumission on the master's entering security for the payment of a certain sum, in case the slave should be disabled from maintaining himself. Now as this depends on a distant contingency, an alteration in the circumstances of the master and his sureties, (if any are required) may effectually disable him or them from making good their engagements. Whereas in the mode I propose, the money due on every manumission which requires it, being paid to a proper officer, remains secure with the publick. And if the slave on whose account it was paid, should never want any assistance, the fund allotted for the purpose will be so much the richer; which is a considerable advantage in its favour.

Some may think it necessary that no manumission should legally operate in all circumstances, beyond a certain age. The difficulty which would generally occur in determining the age of a negro, might be removed by enabling a magistrate to convene three or five men, who, or a majority of them, after hearing such evidence as could be adduced, and judging from appearances, should declare their judgment of his or her age. These, with many other particular considerations, will doubtless be properly attended to, whenever a matter of this consequence, comes under the immediate notice of a legislature. Some difficulty may attend ascertaining with precision the sums which will be necessary to pay, at the respective ages of manumission, to secure the publick from any unjust burden. It is a matter that requires judgment, and a particular kind of calculation with which I am but little acquainted. But as it may further explain what I have suggested; I will venture a few more hints on the subject.

I understand that on emancipating a slave in Pennsylvania, the law requires security should be entered for 30l. without any regard to age, or any other circumstances; and that if the person so emancipated, should afterwards require assistance, any expence exceeding that sum, is paid by the township to which he or she may belong. Although this mode is liable to some exceptions, for reasons before given, I have nAever heard of any burden, arising therefrom, occasioning any uneasiness among the people of that province. Hence we may infer that the sum of 30l. has been generally found sufficient for the purpose. By the Breslau bills of mortality, it is found that the chances are equal, that a man of fifty years of age will live seventeen years. Let us consider what inconveniences might arise, if 20l. was paid on the manumission of a slave of that age, who afterwards lived seventeen years, in the first ten of which, we will suppose he could support himself by his labour; and that in the remaining seven he required assistance, the expence whereof amounted to 30l. which, as before-mentioned, experience has found to be sufficient. Now 20l. put to interest (or applied to the other uses of the fund, which is the same thing) for ten years, at six per centum per annum, amounts to 32l. which leaves a balance in favour of the publick of 2l. besides the interest still arising on the decreasing principle, after the first ten years, and the benefit of his labour; which would further increase that balance. If this calculation is just, (and if it is erroneous, I think the error is in favour of the publick) it will be a publick advantage to permit manumission on these terms; and if it takes place at forty, a much less sum will answer the purpose; and so in a decreasing proportion to the age of twenty-one years, when, as has been before shewn, nothing can be justly expected. Now we find that if, on the manumission of a slave between the years of twenty-one and fifty, fourteen shillings is paid to the publick for every year his or her age exceeds twenty-one, it will bear a very near proportion to 20l. paid on a manumission at fifty, as above stated. I may be mistaken in the method I have taken to determine the sufficiency of that sum; but I am so confident that the community would feel no inconvenience from adopting it, that, had I a sufficient estate to authorize the proposal, I should not fear deriving a considerable advantage from undertaking to support all the negroes so manumitted, who required assistance, with the monies so paid; exclusive of the benefit accruing to the community from their labour, in which I should be only interested as an individual.

Thus I have stated, and proposed a method for settling the account, as it stands, on a manumission, with the publick. There are many who, cheerfully complying with these terms, would also remember that in some cases, there is another account depending between them and their slaves: and any encouragement or assistance they may suppose it their duty to give them in consideration of past services, will still lessen the risque of their ever becoming chargeable to the publick.

To conclude—the object I have proposed, has an undoubted claim to the most serious consideration of people of all ranks, and of every denomination; for justice is confessedly alike obligatory on all. If to relieve the person of a single debtor from a temporary imprisonment, has repeatedly been admitted as a sufficient call for the interposition of a legislature—what is not due to the prosecution of the means of preventing the miseries inseparably attendant on, and the cruelties and deplorable sufferings too often annexed to, a state of perpetual slavery; in which many thousands of our fellow-creatures are, and may be unjustly detained? Let us reconcile our practice to our avowed principles. Let not our professions of an inviolable attachment to liberty, of late so frequently echoed from one end of the continent to the other, be contradicted by a practice as unjust as it is impolitick. Doctor Young is very severe where he says "The world's all title page, there's no contents." Let our conduct shew our title to an exception. Let us therefore immediately consider, and adopt the most prudent measures for relieving those oppressed people; and of enemies make them friends and useful members of society, by confering on them such privileges as will interest them in the general welfare.

Being sensible of my deficiency, I should have been pleased, had the few hints I have presumed to obtrude on the publick, employed a pen more equal to the importance of my subject. Conscious, however, of my motive in giving them, I flatter myself they will meet from the candid, the reception which is due to a good intention. As a wellwisher to the religious and civil interests of my country, I am willing to contribute my mite towards the removal of an evil, which I believe to be dangerous to both: and if any thoughts I have meant to express, have the least tendency to effect it; I shall be indifferent whatever opinion is formed of the dress they appear in.

To the Friends of the Abolition of the Slave Trade

To the Friends of the Abolition of the Slave Trade

The great object of your wishes is t length nearly accomplished. A traffic disgraceful to humanity and odious in the sight of God, has by your persevering efforts been rendered so hateful in the eyes of men, that the people of this country could no longer bear it. There never were two opinions, indeed, upon the subject, among persons whose minds had not been blinded by ignorance or interest. But to you belong the praise of laying open the case before all the world, and urging the truth so unremittingly, that every man who thinks at all now understands the question. The fixed opinion of the public was so strongly in your favour, that the views of interested individuals could no more oppose you. Aided by the honest and enlightened zeal of the late Ministry, you have in the two last Sessions triumphed over the only obstacles that remained, and the first object of your exertions is now obtained, the British Slave Trade is declared illegal – I say the first object, and I am going to explain what I mean.

An act of Parliament has been passed by which the Slave Trade is condemned- but the sentence remains to be executed. This statute enacts that after a certain time no vessels shall be fitted out for the trade in slaves- that after another period all cruisers shall have a right to seize British vessels carrying the slaves. Now in order to enforce these enactments, there must concur the revenue officers in the ports of this country, the commanders of cruizers, and the revenue officers, as well as the governors and commanders in the West Indies. Would you trust much to the zeal of a poor Liverpool tide-waiter in detecting his good friend the rich slave-merchant? Will many persons be found to inform upon the tide-waiter in a town which has lately been mobbing for the lost slave trade? Do you think the captains of ships likely of themselves to hunt out delinquents, when almost all the seamen who gave evidence upon the slave trade, were so fond of it, that they spoke not like witnesses but advocates?

Then, what think you of the West-Indians themselves for spies upon their own conduct, and informs against the breakers of so hated a law? When these are the persons to whom of necessity is left the charge of seeing this act carried into effect – my notion is that we cannot expect to see it executed at all, unless we continue to watch them close. We must not leave the whole of our measure in their hands, at the most critical moment of all, after we have carried it on to the very point of succeeding, in spite of their teeth. We must keep a vigilant eye upon them and upon [any] who may be likely to take part with them, or give them protection, else we have done nothing. We have carried a piece of written paper from one house of Parliament to the other, and then printed it- but we have not prevented the Liverpool traders from carrying thousands of negroes over to the West Indies, and there selling them to be tortured and murdered.

It is peculiarly necessary for you to keep these things in mind at this moment, when the election of a new parliament is going on. It never was so important for our cause to have abolitionists chosen as the representatives and rulers of this country. Even if the ministers who helped us to carry through the Abolition Act had remained in Office – I would say – "Take care to elect men who will steadily watch over its execution." But unfortunately for our great question, in consequence of misunderstandings which neither you nor I have any thing to do with, those ministers are turned out, and another set of men are brought into their places, whom we know to be among our greatest enemies. Except one or two individuals of no great influence in the government, and still less weight in the country, the whole of the new ministry are decided and violent enemies of the Abolition – What chance have we then of seeing it carried into effect, but by redoubling our own zeal in watching over those ministers – in finding out the breaches of the act which will infallibly take place – and above all in chusing such representatives as may most strenuously help us, both in looking after the ministry and in seeing the bill enforced.

It is a very common thing for worthy abolitionists to ask a candidate before giving him their votes, what his opinions are upon the slave trade? to which he generally answers – he is an abolitionist. – But I say this is not enough in these times. He may be an abolitionist in his heart, and yet do us no good. We must have men who are both right in their opinions, and zealous in supporting them – men who will go a greater length to serve our cause than merely calling themselves "abolitionists." We must chuse such as will fight stoutly for us – and, if possible, such as can fight well and win the day.

There is another thing which I wish you to consider well, both now and after the election is over, but especially at the present moment – and it is better deserving of your attention because you have not heretofore had an opportunity of reflecting much upon it. The abolition of the British Slave Trade will free us from our own share of the guilt. But while certain foreign nations continue to carry on their slave trade our's can never be completely stopt: and even if it could, Africa would still be subject in a great degree to the horrors which this detestable traffic constantly produces. The war has suspended the Slave Trade of France and Holland. But Portugal carries it on to an enormous amount. More slaves are transported from Africa to the Portuguese colonies, and through them to the Spanish, than we ourselves have been in the practice of sending to our West India Islands. Can nothing be done to prevail upon the government of Portugal that this horrible commerce shall be given up? We have nearly as great influence there as Bonaparte has in Holland. And I am sure that if he chose to make his Dutch allies oblige him by humoring some of his vicious caprices, he would find them quite well disposed to oblige him. I doubt not he might pick out and take a province or two if he chose: and for a few millions more or less of contribution, they would not much care to quarrel with him. Why should we be unable to do as handsomely for the cause of humanity and justice, with our dependent allies, as Bonaparte does every day with his, for lucre of grain, and the gratification of his unnatural ambition? Trust me we should find it a very easy matter to get the Portuguese Slave Trade abolished – if we set about it as we ought. Let the ministers only use the influence which they have over an ally whom this country has supported by fleets, armies and treasures, for years and years. They will put an end to the only branch of the Slave Trade that now remains, while they promote the execution of our own law. And I am sure no good man will then regret the sums that have been spent during our Portuguese connexion.

But "a peace will come, the French, Dutch and Spanish Slave Trade will revive" I do sincerely hope we shall once more have peace – because I am deeply persuaded that we do no good by continuing the war. But this matter is foremost to our purpose – Only I must observe that let the negotiations for peace begin when they may, it is of essential consequence to the cause of abolition that our friends should at that time have weight in the government. Let us trust that the ministers of the day, when the next offer of peace is made, will keep steadily in their view of necessity of inducing the enemy and his allies to give up the slave trade – or at least to concur with us in such an agreement as may secure the safety of our own abolition. I should tremble indeed, to see a peace with France negotiated by any but abolitionists. As, however, the present ministers are unfortunately for us, friendly to the Slave

Trade, we must be doubly zealous in surrounding them with faithful representatives, who will scrupulously watch over their conduct at the important period of which I am speaking, and will see that the cause of abolition suffers no injury from being trusted to its enemies.

In a word, it is your duty now to choose such men as will zealously carry the British Abolition Act into effect – promote the extension of this virtuous measure to our allies over whom we have full influence – and be ready to plead the same cause when ministers shall be disposed to treat with France for peace. But chuse whom you will as representatives – you must continue your own persevering exertions, and recollect that your object is not accomplished while the act remains to be executed – while Portugal carries thousands of slaves by our permission yearly from Africa – while a peace remains to be made, which shall determine the restoration of the termination of the enemy's Slave Trade – above all, while the government of this country is in the hands of the persons most averse to abolition. Reflect on these things at the present moment – and do not dismiss them form your thoughts until you have turned them to the profit of our great and righteous cause.

A Brother Abolitionist

A Letter on the Greater Necessity of an Abolition of the African Slave Trade

A Letter on the Greater Necessity of an Abolition of the African Slave Trade; In Consequence of the Insurrection at St. Domingo, &c.

By a Gentleman Long Resident in Jamaica

Extracted from the Universal Museum, No. 3, just published. Prefaced by a Short Address to the Publick, by W. Matthews

Bath:
Printed by R. Crutwell
1792.
Price One Penny.

On The Slave Trade.

To the Publick.

The following Letter is written in a style of candour and argument, which it is presumed will recommend it to the attentive consideration of every reader, desirous to hear the voice of truth. The time is approaching when, most probably, the great and solemn question of the Abolition of the Slave Trade will again come under Parliamentary discussion; and it is much to be wished that every well-informed and benevolent man, desirous of offering his opinion founded on his knowledge of facts, may be previously heard. With this view, the letter had been printed for distribution by some Friends of the Abolition, who, in so styling themselves, humbly trust they assume no title that should not be common; no distinction but that of friends of their country, and of human kind. In the present crisis, they must consider themselves as peculiarly accountable to the Searcher of hearts, the Righteous Judge of all men, for the part they take, and for the language they hold, under a firm persuasion that found policy and indispensible righteousness call aloud for an Abolition. Between truth and error there can be no medium – between a barbarous policy and continual danger, no security – between publick oppression and publick guilt, no extenuation – between grinding cruelty and crying sin, no possible distinction. The approaching day of another decision on a question so awfully involved – a question on the issue of which may depend the wretchedness or comparative comfort, of millions of fellow-beings, is a day of no common concern! Every serious man must look towards it with anxiety – and feel an increasing solicitude for a favourable event; and he must deprecate a protraction of that event, as a continuation of national infamy and horror.

While these sentiments necessarily agitate the publick mind, a strong presumption indeed comes in favour of the so-much-desired abolition. Since the late investigation by evidence before the Committee of Parliament, the subject has undergone a more general and more close attention than ever. A detail of the most solemn and indubitable evidence can have left but little doubt in their nation, respecting the abominable cruelty of the present system. Such has been the effect on the minds of a generous people, that few individuals can be found who would not be willing to sacrifice, if sacrifice were necessary, some private emolument to the general cause of justice and humanity. But sacrifices of any valuable interest, do not now appear to be wanted. The subject, stripped of error and sophistry, is now better understood. The chief sacrifices to be made are those unprincipled rapacity in a few individuals, whose eyes have been blinded and whose minds have been distorted, by the delusive influence of the God of this world. If, in the extreme of supposition, the interested arguments of such men, who covet the precarious advantages of an infamous traffick, were to be allowed for a moment to have any weight; the degree of it must be tried in opposition to the immutable principles of honour, justice, and benignity; and, brought into such a comparison, the arguments of *Slave Traders* would surely be but as dust in the balance, and unworthy of regard! But when on the broad basis of a found and righteous policy, every fair and rational argument is against the miserable maxims of such men, their complaints, if they dare any longer to urge them, should be treated by every good man with a righteous indignation. If the commerce in slaves (ruinous as it sometimes proves) were attended with no more than an ordinary profit, in connexion with the system of selling to the planters, the sanguinary and calamitous consequences are too diabolical to be sported with. If, on the contrary, the price of blood has accumulated by inhuman individuals, and their families have been supported by it in a baneful voluptuousness, let the pangs of devoted innocence, let the dying agonies of innumerable victims, at length be heard in their proper language: - "Think the measure of our miseries, and of your abominations sufficiently full, O BARBARIANS! – be satisfied, O CHRISTIANS!"

The field of honourable commerce is wide and open – even larger than sufficient to employ all the active ingenuity, and to supply all the wants of man! Within those bounds may it be the glorious prerogative of a British Parliament, to restrain the efforts of the British subjects! On such principles it is impossible that a commercial people should be unhappy or oppressed, or inferior on the scale of nations; - but on the principles of systematic cruelty, any country must not only be inglorious, but the instruments and the subjects eternal calamity!

W. M.

Arguements for Abolishing the African Slave Trade

To the Editor of the Universal Museum,

Sir,

I rejoice to find that the abolition of that iniquitous and disgraceful traffick, the *African Slave Trade*, is again in agitation, and have no doubt when the people of this country come to have a right idea of the subject, that it will meet with better success than in the late decision of parliament. The recent calamities in the French islands is a fresh proof of the necessity there is for putting an immediate stop to this trade. Let not the opposers of the abolition exult at this event, as the consequence of Mr. Wiberforce's delusive philanthropy, as it is called; the day may not be very distant when the same ' enes may be reacted in our islands, should we continue to pour in such multitudes of negroes as are annually imported into our islands, considering their weak state, and the little attention paid to population among the whites. Every importation is an importation of so many enemies, who will eventually overrun the islands, should the increase of whites not keep pace. Hitherto, for want of a right idea upon the subject, a great part of the people of this country have considered that by the abolition of the African Slave Trade was meant the emancipation of the slaves in our colonies, which they conceived was big with mischief, injustice, and ruin. Such it would be; but it is necessary to inform them that the emancipation of the colonies was never meant, and that it is necessary they should separate in their minds and make a proper distinction between two of the things. The Abolition then of the *African* Slave Trade, that is, the importing of slaves from Africa into our islands, which it appears from a multiplicity of incontrovertible evidence is not now any longer necessary, either for the existence of the colonies or the farther extention of them, is what is meant; for it is a certain fact that the islands have of late years so much increased in population, that if now the aid of cattle and machinery, which were never used to any extent before, were called in, it would more than compensate for any deficiency from a non-importation of slaves from Africa; and nothing will oblige the planter to bring cattle and machinery into general use, but the stopping of this trade. The people of this country, among other pretexts set up, have been amused with the idle tale that the plough could not be used in the islands; it is a fact, that wherever it has been used the crops have been abundant, the labour of the slaves lessened nearly one half, and the planter enriched. The soil and situation of that part of the world is much the same as this; high and low lands, vallies, hills, and mountains; but some people artfully cry out, How can you plough the mountains? These are unnecessary for the sugar estates, and may be converted to purposes equally useful, such as provision, cotton, coffee, &c. There is another objection set up by the planters, That the sexes are not equal for the purposes of propagation: this will always exist if the importing of slaves continued; for the planter will ever buy more men than women – present gain, and not the interest of posterity, being considered; the men being better calculated to dig cane holes, (which cattle and the plough ought to do) and endure hard labour, than the women; so that what they set up as an excuse, will continue to exist if the trade is permitted.* Another plea set up by the planters is, That the condition of the negroe is happier in our islands than in his own country. Nothing surely could ever be more insulting to reason and repugnant to truth, than this assertion. It is a fact which no sophistry can controvert, that his situation is happier in his own country than abroad. If it were not so, he would rejoice to be taken away, and at the change; he would give no resistance during the voyage, but look forward with cheerful hope for happiness in a different land, which was denied him in his own: But the contrary of this is the case, else why do they chain the men on board? – This argument alone is sufficient to confute the idle tale, that they are happier and more reconciled; necessity alone reconciles them, so far as they are reconciled. Is it not natural to suppose, that if they led the miserable life in Africa, we have been told they do, that they would rejoice at being taken away? On the contrary, we see them, particularly those advanced in life, pine away with grief, and even make away with themselves, in the firm hope of returning to their own country, and to their friends in the state they are in, and in this hope cheerfully meet death! Let any one contradict this, who is in the least conversant with the islands!

----

* The merchants and planners at their meeting at the London Tavern of the 3d and 5th of November, say, Resolution 11th, "That their slaves are happy under their present masters, &c. and under the assurance of additional relief when requisite, by a continuance of seasonable importations from Africa, &c." Lucry, Would it not have been better to have said, "By the introduction and general use of cattle and the plough to lessen their labour?"

On this account partly the planter purchasing young people, as in the young and thoughtless despondency does not take that root, and they sooner forget their cares. As a farther proof that they do not meet with those punishments in their own country that are inflicted upon them in our islands, I never saw among new Negroes the marks of stripes or whipping, which is so common among those in the islands; and I have known them so simple and ignorant of this sort of punishment, viz. castigation, that when first taken to be flogged, they have not known what it meant, until they felt the lash. It is also the general opinion among them, that they are kidnapped or stolen: nay, even the Assembly of Jamaica have admitted this in their two Reports. They say, in Report 1st, 'That it is the opinion of tis committee, that the wisdom and authority of parliament might be beneficially exerted in the further regulations of the African commerce, in preventing the detention of ships upon the coast, in prohibiting the purchase of slaves, who shall appear to have been kidnapped, or deprived liberty contrary to the usage and custom of Africa, &c." – Here it is admitted, that many are stolen, and that they enjoy liberty in Africa. The tender care professed here by a Jamaican House of Assembly for the rights and liberties of the natives of Africa, is too extraordinary a circumstance to escape the observation of the reader.

Those who have given any attention to the publications of the use, propriety, and justice of the Slave Trade, will have observed, that of those who defend the benefit, right and justice, the most able, that is, the most artful, perceiving the impossibility of justifying our making slaves, or the encouraging others in the making of slaves of those who are born in a state of natural or political freedom, either deny that the natives of Africa have such rights, or alledge that they have forfeited them to the laws of their country by crimes, the punishment of which is slavery. Some describe the governments in Africa to be universally pure despotism, or they argue as if they supposed them to be such, and conclude that the state of slavery in the British colonies is so much preferable to the condition our slaves were removed from, that the change is a real blessing. Long, on this subject [see chap. i. ii. iii. B. 3d of the 2d vol. of his History of Jamaica, under the head Negroes,] determined to lay a solid foundation for the wicked conclusions he intended to draw, supposes them scarcely, if at all, superior to brute beasts; the conclusion from which is, that they were meant for the slaves of men, white men to be sure, or Indians; for, according to Mr.

Long, Negroes are hardly men. Then having reasoned them down to a level with the Ourang-Outangs; or rather the Ourangs up to, or above the Negroes; he proceeds to state, that their government is so arbitrary, and their condition so absolutely slavish, that it is a great melioration of their state, to transfer to the condition of slavery, them and their posterity, in Jamaica or the other islands.

Now we see it is admitted that there are free people in Africa, and an anxious care (risuan teneatis!) is taken by the legislature of Jamaica, to observe that the rights of those free men shall not be infringed, lest it draw the good people of Jamaica into the dreadful predicament of having bought as slaves those who had a right to freedom. Now, if one who has seen how negroes are sold on board a Guinea-ship, were to read this passage of the Reports, and were to ask those conscientious Committee-men this question, "You see, gentlemen, how very necessary it is to guard against the kidnapping of free people of Africa, and until some care shall be taken in that particular, by the wisdom and authority of the British parliament, pray how do you intend to guard yourself from partaking in the same guilt with the kidnapper? How have you guarded against it hitherto? I suppose you took with you a linguist, and examined those you intended to buy some days before the sale; or if that could not be, for it is impossible at the sale, then I suppose on taking them home, you went through the necessary scrutiny, and upon finding that the negroe was born free, and had not forfeited his right to freedom by committing felony, of course you restored him to that liberty, of which he was unjustly deprived." I say, were any men seriously to put this question to the very men who framed that clause, they would laugh in his face. Let me speak out: - A sensible writer, whose sentiments I have given, says, 'That clause, and several others in the bill, are merely held out to amuse the people at large in England; but in Jamaica has no meaning;' and I quote it to show the low artifices which even a legislative body are obliged to stoop to, when to suppress what is true, and to affect what has no existence, becomes necessary to support the cause they are advocates for.

Among other curious clauses in these Reports, is the following: 'It seems not to be understood in Great Britain, that the inhabitants of the West-India islands have no concern in the ships trading to Africa: the African trade is purely a British trade, carried on by British subjects residing in Great-britain, on capitals of their own; the connexion and intercourse between the planters of this island, and the merchants of

Great-Britain trading to Africa, extend no further than the mere purchase of what *British acts* have declared to be *legal* subjects of purchase.'
Here then, it would seem, that the islands take no part in, and with to
exculpate themselves from the odium of this abominable traffick, and
cast it on the merchants,* and British acts of parliament! – but which
is worse, the receiver or the thief? They have no concern in it, - if so,
should parliament hesitate for a moment in casting off this odium from
a free people, take the islands at their word, and cut it up, as being
unnecessary? These, and many other clauses, shew to what shifts the
Assembly of Jamaica was reduced, to wipe away an odium they could
not but acknowledge. Btu in every step they stumbled; and if any man
will read these reports attentively, he will agree with me, that they have
admitted every thing that this country has charged them with, and that
their interference was necessary.

I shall now, Mr. Editor, endeavour to point out a few of the advantages, among a great many, that will accrue to the planter, and rest
it upon its utility.

It is surprising, and yet it is not the first instance, to see men opposing their own interest in the manner the planters have done in join-
ing with the merchants in an opposition. It will prove the most advantageous thing to them on many accounts, and they know it; but such
is the influence of the merchants to whom the planter is in debt, and
looking for further loans, that he has no voice of his own; indeed, in
their present situation (with but few exceptions) they are mere *nominal*
holders of property; the merchants of this country having generally
mortgages to a great amount on their estates, and this is in a great measure owing to the African trade, as the planter is perpetually running in
debt for negroes, in hopes of extending his views; for they have, in the
earlier settlements of the island, (I speak of Jamaica, the great object)
taken up and *monopolized* large tracts of King's land which they have
in view of settling or day or other with Africans, but which are now
useless. Nothing has been more injurious hitherto to the settling of
Jamaica, than this monopoly; it has prevented the smaller settler from
improving lands, and settling penns, (grass farms) which are of the
utmost utility to the island, for they are settled with little labour and

---

* In their 3d Revolution of the 8th of Nov. the merchants and planters assert, that they have been urged and stimulated to this trade under sanction
of the legslature, and by its repeated acts and declarations. What is this but
casting the whole of the odium upon this country?

expence in comparison with sugar estates, which require large capitals; but the small settler has been prevented from this by the proprietors of sugar estates holding large tracts of land, which they will neither sell (while the quit-rents remain so low) nor settle.

There are a variety of settlements, the produce of which would contribute to the trade of this country, as well as sugar, that are settled and carried on at a small expence and labour, such as cotton, coffee, &c. Besides, by extending their grass penns, abundance of hides might be sent to this country, where they are become extremely dear. All these kind of settlements, I repeat, are made with little expence; an industrious man, with a few negroes, will, in a short time, open a vast deal of land for grazing; for, when once opened and plan ted in Guinea grass, it requires little else than tilling the pastures annually to keep them in order. Another great advantage that would arise to the planter in this way, would be the great increase, and consequent cheapness of cattle for carrying on the sugar estates; and such would be the plenty, that their negroes might be fed in part, if not wholly, with meat instead of salted herrings, which would hearten up their slaves, and give them strength and power to do more, and that with a willing mind; for when the body is well supported, the mind becomes capable of great exertions, without goading and whipping, (too disgraceful a mode of exciting men to labour.) We want no logic to prove this; every man knows it; - nay, the very brutes (if I may be allowed the expression) that are necessary for labour, know it.

These and many more advantages will arise from the abolition of the Slave Trade; but while that trade continues, such is the rage for sugar estates, that the old system will remain, and new estates must be settled by negroes, as ploughs cannot be used with ease in the new tilled lands, on account of the stumps of the trees left in the ground to decay.

We have at present sugar estates enough settled to give this kingdom, and even others, as much sugar as can be consumed, at a *moderate* price. As a proof of this, witness that our islands are now, and since the dissentions in the French islands have been, supplying the Continent with sugars. Where then is the use of, or necessity for, our settling any more sugar estates, but to gratify the vanity and ambition of individuals? Are not cotton, coffee, and other articles, as useful to the commerce of this country as sugar, which it has been proved cannot be raised at so easy an expence? Besides, it would give elbow-room to people of small capitals to settle, and consequently population among the whites will increase, which is much wanted both for internal and external defence, and shews the wretched policy heretofore prevailing in that island. There has been a great defect in the system of that island, in not encouraging the small settler, owing to the above monopoly of land. What made Barbadoes at one time so populous; what brought America to the pitch it is, but an attention to this? For want of this, Jamaica is beholden to this country for *internal* protection against their slaves, whom they have been often in dread of, and by whom they have been more than once upon the verge of being destroyed; but had they a numerous and well-regulated militia, this could never happen, and this can only be effected by an attention to the population among the whites; the great source for which will be the encouraging the small settler, by giving him an opportunity to purchase land. If this be not attended to, and fresh recruits of slaves are continued to pour in, I am too much afraid that, one day or other, we may fatally experience the same scenes that are now acting in St. Domingo. God forbid! I hope the planter's eyes will be opened to his own interest, and instead of blaming Mr. W. for a delusive philanthropy, take measures to prevent the fatal catastrophe.

Mr. W. has not produced the dissentions in France, nor did any act of his induce the slaves in Jamaica to rebellion, from whence it was a miracle that the whites escaped, long before the abolition was thought of, or at least seriously taken up.

Another advantage that will arise from the abolition is, that many disorders which the negroes bring with them, will cease; that destructive disorder the yaws, which is kept alive by the importation of new negroes, would cease, and in time be as little heard of as the sweating-sickness; for in some of the old settled parishes, particularly Vere, where new negroes are not so much mixed with the old, it is hardly heard of.

You see, Sir, I have considered myself chiefly to the *advantages* (all of which I have not enumerated) that will arise to the planter from the abolition, without dwelling upon the iniquity of the traffic; and if so many advantages will arise, which cannot be denied, and so much good done, why hesitate a moment in doing away a trade so disgraceful to humanity as this is? Is it that we are afraid it will hurt the revenue of this country, or is the *landed* interest in danger? This was an artful insinuation of Colonel Tarleton, and a masterly stroke; and I am afraid I was the grand charm to fascinate humanity – it was *argumentum ad pecuniam*! Touch my purse, you touch my honour! But is British humanity come to this, to be subservient to interest, and the artful stratagems of a few slave merchants?

Let me conclude by telling the people of this country, particularly the ladies, the fairest part of the creation, who sip their tea, and prattle round their tea-board, that the blood of the poor African, and not that of bullocks, (metaphorically speaking) refines the sugar, which is so grateful to the palate as to lull to sleep the noblest virtue of the mind, Humanity.

A FRIEND TO HIS COUNTRY.

P.S. It has been said that white men cannot cultivate the lands in the islands – this I have my doubts about; but I will tell the planter what work white men may do. They can do all kinds of mechanical work, and take the places of the negroe artisans, who may be turned into the field; but this the planter will object to as a thing he cannot afford, because negroe tradesmen cost him but little. Indeed such has been the avarice and wretched policy of them, that they have often evaded and suffered almost to die away the Deficiency Act, an act manifestly made for the preservation of the island, by keeping a sufficient number of white men upon the estates; to evade this, I have known people given in who lived miles from the estate, and hardly ever upon it: But if they were to employ white tradesmen to reside constantly on the estates, such as masons, carpenters, smiths, mill-wrights, &c. they would always have a body of men ready to act upon any emergency. Instead of this an overseer, and two, three or four book-keepers, are all the white people upon an estate, with two or three hundred blacks. Can there be any wonder if these people are some day or other cut off?people given in who lived miles from the estate, and hardly ever upon it: But if they were to employ white tradesmen to reside constantly on the estates, such as masons, carpenters, smiths, mill-wrights, &c. they would always have a body of men ready to act upon any emergency. Instead of this an overseer, and two, three or four book-keepers, are all the white people upon an estate, with two or three hundred blacks. Can there be any wonder if these people are some day or other cut off?

Hints for a Specific Plan for an Abolition of the Slave Trade

Hints for a Specific Plan for an Abolition of the Slave Trade, and for Relief of the Negroes in the British West Indies.

By the Translator of Cicero's Orations against Verres.

LONDON:
Printed for J. Debrett, in Piccadilly.
M3DCC3LXXXVIII

Advertisement.

Many publications have of late appeared for and against the slave trade. I trust, however, that it will not be denied that the worthy persons who have employed their pens in behalf of the present system, (impartial planters, candid African merchants, humane apologists for Negro slavery, &c. &c.) have been spirited up in its defense by the ardent and active principle of private interest, notwithstanding their avowed anxiety for the publick happiness and grandeur; and that, on the other hand, they whose writings recommend an abolition, or even a modification of this detestable commerce, can have nothing at heart but the honour, the virtue, the security of the empire. They could gain nothing, by such a measure, but the welfare of Britain and of mankind; while they have much to lose, if (as their adversaries exclaim) it should occasion a general mischief to the community. – Whether this circumstance may not tend to weaken the arguments on one side, and to strengthen the cause on the other, is submitted to the judgment of the reader.

Hints, &c.

Every man who is zealous for the zealous for the rights and happiness of human kind, must feel himself anxious for the fate of the question concerning the slave trade, which is shortly to undergo a parliamentary discussion: a question, to which the partial interests of individuals are expected to create vigourous opposition.

Several pamphlets have fallen into my hands, befriending this system of inveterate barbarity. In one of them, which was published some years ago, and is now republished, relative to the cause of Somerset and Knowles, I could not help being surprised at certain dogmas in justification and defense of the Negro trade in general. They appear not only unwarranted by reason, but even deficient in point of humanity. The writer of that pamphlet hath armed himself with an act of parliament, which it is difficulty to reconcile to the spirit of the constitution, to natural justice, to the dictates of found policy, to the precepts of Christianity. We cannot read, without pain and sorrow, of millions of our fellow-creatures considered by law as articles of commerce, like the produce of the foil, or the beast of the field. The writer already mentioned, speaking of Mr. Stewart, the gentleman who claimed Somerset the Negro as his property, says, "If the return had set forth that Mr. Stewart had brought him here as an article of commerce, with some elephants teeth, wax, and leather, and under the sanction of the laws of trade: that he meant to export him hence under the same protection, with his other property, in order to be sold for his better advantage in one of the English colonies in America: that a writ of Habeas Corpus might as well issue on account of his elephants teeth, wax, and his leather, and his commodities, as on account of his Negro, they being expressly under the same predicament of law, and so forth: I say, under such circumstances, and upon such a return, what would have become of this stately pile of elaborate argument?"*

After which, relinquishing the word slavery (it being an odious term), he metaphorically "removes the situation of the cafe, changes its point of view, and rests it on the land of Commercial Property; from whence, "perhaps, it will be seen in a less offensive light, &c." – Having rated them as merchandize, as bales of goods, and confounded them with elephants, teeth, wax and leather, he pleads the act of 5ᵗʰ Geo. II c. 7. and informs us that <u>Negro slaves are</u> "estates and hereditaments,

* Mr. Hargrave's excellent arguments in that cause.

33

assets and property, liable to, and chargeable with all just debts, duties, and demands whatsoever; and that herein there is not a trace of the idea of slavery." – No; for assuming a gentler appellation, it calls itself traffic.

And now, having degraded them by act of parliament from the rank of human beings, he endeavours to reconcile our feelings to their condition, by gravely employing near twenty pages to prove that these unhappy chattels are destitute of the moral sense; at least, that they have it not in any perfection; and that, from the nature of their noses, and the colour of their skin, they are peculiarly selected for slavery by their Creator. He insists, moreover, that the dullness of their intellects is another good reason for devoting these wretched Africans to perpetual bondage, and for making servitude hereditary. If this be a just cause for enslaving our fellow-creatures, with equal reason, and with equal equity, may every stupid person in Great Britain and Ireland be shipped off, and disposed of for money in the colonies. Why not an act of the Legislature authorizing all dunces to be exported from time to time, and sold in the West Indies as a community, a species of traffic, and to be as assets and property, and elephants teeth, in the scale of things. It would be no inconvenient measure, either for the colonies, or for another country. The kingdom would be disburthened of many able-bodied blockheads, and the duty on exportation would advantage the revenue.

But what right have we to interpret for the Almighty? This is aggravating our crime, and impudently apologizing for avarice by impiety. Upon the same principle may every successful act of violence be justified. We have no more right to trade with the persons of the people of Guinea, than with those the natives of Otaheite or New Holland. From whence did the British parliament derive the power of sanctioning such wickedness, and calling it Commerce? The act that permitted it, should be expunged from the journals, if we hope to subsist as a great and a happy people.

This alledged deficiency in the mental powers was the pretext of Cortez and his sanguinary followers, for the cruelties inflicted on the natives of the New World. The Indians were represented to the court of Spain as a race of beings but little removed from brutes, and as such, only, formed to labour for their conquerors, and be employed in the room of beasts of burthen. Yet were there found some who supported their cause, who vindicated their faculties, and pleaded so forcibly with the parent state, that that just and enlightened minister, Cardinal Ximenes, was preparing to punish those oppressors of mankind, and to frame a code of laws which should in the future protect America, when his death disappointed her of the benefits expected from the humane and upright, the vigourous and decisive measures which marked the administration of that incomparable statesman. To this may be added that splendid exertion of pontifical authority by Pope Paul the Third; who, when Charles the Fifth had doomed the natives of the new hemisphere to slavery, issued out a bull that restored them to liberty. But there were inefficient efforts against human avidity, and Spain dates her downfall from execrable æra of her Indian victories.

Another palliating argument, equally extraordinary, is, that numbers of the lower class in Britain experience from poverty more real wretchedness, than the slaves in the West Indies endure from servitude. But what an argument! Does our own wretchedness entitle us to extend it to others? – Our miners are next compared to the Negroes for misery. There is no parallel here. The miners in England work, with their own consent, for stated wages, and may, if they think proper, abandon their occupation. The impressing of seamen, says the author of the pamphlet already alluded to, is likewise an instance in which slavery hath been countenanced by the Legislature of this kingdom. I contend that the cases are in no way similar. Seamen are never impressed, but to answer the urgent necessities of the state: the slave trade is always in being. Seamen suffer but a temporary restraint: the bondage of Negroes is for life. The seaman is well paid, and, if he is killed in the service, his children are protected and maintained by the nation: is there any thing like this in the condition of a Negro? No, he is an inferior link in the chain of creation, he is barely equivalent to wax, and leather, and elephants teeth; he is assets and property.

The author of a discourse, intitled, "An Apology for Negro Slavery," after having spoken most contemptuously of the people called Quakers, for their benevolent endeavours to eradicate this grievance, insists that the Negroes are far from being unhappy. According to him, when they arrive at the plantations, it is quite a party of pleasure. They there meet many of their countrymen whom they knew very well in Africa, and are glad to shake hands with their old acquaintances. In the evening they have a dance, and, from the flattering accounts they receive from their partners, are impatient to be sold the next morning. Will any man of reflection subscribe to such assertions? It is a fact well known, that many of the settlements are harassed and laid waste by wandering armies of the fugitive Negroes. In Jamaica there is a republic of them. The great swamps in the Carolinas harbour thousands that have fled from the horrours of inexorable despotism. If these are the only proofs that can be given of their felicity, the slaves in our colonies are the most miserable of mortals.

But the Negro trade is justifiable, because the Blacks are, in their native country, sunk (says the Apologist) in the vilest state of barbarism: because their laws are absurd, their religion abominable. Even granting that this is true, hath it ever been proved that they are incapable of receiving any benefit from instruction? If they are not incapable, to buy them and sell them, as a marketable commodity, is no eligible method of improving their understandings. Slavery debases and corrupts the human mind. Before we came amongst them, the inhabitants of Guinea were only savages: but we are destroying even the hope of their being civilized, and rendering their condition irremediable.

The Jesuits in Paraguay and California, instead of procuring from the crown of Spain a license to ship off and vend the natives, exerted their talents and indefatigable industry to teach those wandering tribes the worship of a God, and the comforts of a civil society. The enterprize was fortunate: they have succeeded, in spite of innumerable obstacles: in the vast solitudes of the Western hemisphere they have introduced humanity, and persuaded the rude Indian to exchange a savage freedom for the blessings of a peaceful and salutary subordination.

We have not only authorized, encouraged and established slavery in our own external territories, but have likewise been the cause of its progress and continuation in countries not subject to our dominion. No sooner was it known in Africa that slaves were an object of commerce to Europeans, than it became the interest and occupation of the princes of those regions to provide us with a regular and ample supply. Endless wars were waged by the Negro nations, with no other intent but the acquisition of captives. The slightest misdemeanours were punished with loss of freedom; and fraud and violence were the ways and means of raising the necessary complement for this traffic. Thus, by a strange and shocking concurrence of wicked circumstances, Britain, that boasts of being the residence of Liberty, a land so favoured and exalted by Heaven, is destroying in remote kingdoms that freedom she adores at home, and spreading slaughter and slavery from one hemisphere to the other.

What is the life of a Negro slave? He first experiences the rigours of captivity in his native country – is at length sold, and, with some hundreds more, stowed in the dark and noisome hold of an African trader. (I say nothing of the horrid usage to the Women slaves on board.) If he survives the effects of sickness, inquietude, ferocious treatment, and bad food, he is exhibited, often half famished, in open market in some island of the West Indies – is disposed of to (frequently) an inhuman master – is branded with an iron – treated with perpetual contumely – kept to extreme and unremitting labour – scourged by a brutal overseer – would even, perhaps, be crucified, if his tyrants dared in a country professing Christianity!

To the infinite scandal of our character as a nation, not only the Negroes endure more misery in our colonies, than in other West Indian islands, but even in the management of the trade which supplies them, is British brutality become proverbial. I will cite a cafe which came before the Court of King's Bench in England, and is reported in II. Burrow. The captain of a ship which was freighted with Negroes, having found, on arriving at the place of his destination, that the market was over, thought fit to steer for some other port. By his own improvidence the vessel had been put barely victualed for her voyage to the island she had lately touched at. Alarmed at the idea of the distress he might suffer, before the ship could reach the market she was then bound for, he determines to obviate the mischief by thinning his cargo, which consisted of about two or three hundred Negroes. In consequence of his diabolic resolution, the barbarian ordered seventy of them to be brought upon the deck, by two at a time, chained together, and in this condition to be thrown overboard. Several of these poor wretches, in attempting to clamber up the ship's sides, had their hands chopped off by persons stationed at the gunwale for that purpose. The point for the decision of the Court was, whether this was such a loss as would render the Insurers liable.

Let us now consider the question in a political light. The employing slaves instead of hired servants, hath ever been accounted as an unwise measure. If slaves, says Aristotle, are treated with severity, revolt will follow; if with indulgence, they become ungovernable, and look upon themselves as on an equality with their masters. Slaves cannot lose the sense of their ignominious condition, nor the remembrance of past miseries. They will sigh for that freedom which every human being prizes, and will struggle to regain it by sedition and massacre.

Totidem nobis hostes esse, quot servos, was a well-known proverb of the ancients. The histories of Greece and Rome abound with examples of insurrection and outrage by those exasperated wretches.* Formidable by their numbers, provoked by injuries, and stimulated by a thirst of revenge, they gave no quarter; and the dungeon and the cross, by an awful retaliation, became the terrour and destruction of their merciless oppressors.

A multitude of slaves (and vast is the multitude in the colonies) is, at all times, a mischief alarming to a community. It is peculiarly dangerous in the New World, from the glaring dissimilitude between the Blacks and the white people. A Roman senator once opposed a law for distinguishing the different orders of their dress, from an apprehension that the slaves might, by such a measure, be struck with the greatness of their own strength.

Slavery impairs the real force of the colonies. If an invasion be expected, those who, as slaves, are always doubtful, frequently terrible inmates, would, if free, become the great bulwark of the islands. At present, an enemy cab, by means of the Negroes, create a diversion: even the first enterprize of an aspiring individual would be to offer them the cap of liberty.

Another mischief (which springs out of the foregoing) is, that the greater the number of slaves, the more violent must be the severities exercised upon them. The growth of the one evil necessarily involves the growth of the other. As your plantations extend, your slaves must be augmented. When the disproportion is so vast, you must balance your weakness by additional barbarities. Thus iniquity must be keep pace with the progress of our prosperity, and as we flourish in commerce, we increase in cruelty.

Contrary to the usual effects of misfortune, the calamities which have ravaged the Caribbee islands have produced no reformation in their callous proprietors. Their own sufferings, one would think, might have humanized their breasts, and taught them the virtue of compassion. The Negro is not undeserving of pity: his sensibility is exquisite; for, as the sagacious Abbé Raynal remarks, he is affected by music to an extraordinary degree. But the love of domineering is a vice inherent

---

* Amongst others, those of the *Helotes* against the Spartan republic: that headed by *Appius Herdonius*, at Rome, and recorded by *Livy*, lib. Iii. – the war of *Spartacus* the gladiator – the revolt of the slaves in Sicily; for which see Cicero, in the fifth of his Orations against *Verres*.

in the heart of man, and should be subdued by every method that legislation can devise. It is evident, from the subject now before us, how
much the most siagitious abuse of the superiority may pass unregarded,
by having become habitual. It is well known that the Europeans, born
and educated in the West Indies, acquire such habits of domestic domination, as must insensibly extend themselves to publick concerns, and
should be carefully discouraged under a free constitution. The young
Creole, from his tenderest years, is taught to play the tyrant: the imperious infant is often entertained by torturing little Negroes.* Is this a fit
person to be intrusted, at a future day, with the care of our liberties in a
British House of Commons? Exclude him from a seat in that assembly,
as you would a butcher from a serving on a jury.[†]

If any thing could justify, or even palliate the oppression of the slave
trade, it must be a situation of extreme necessity. But those amongst
the planters who have written to defend it, argue one while, as if the
question was solely the expediency or inexpediency of an abolition
with respect to the sugar trade, and the profits of proprietors; industri-
ously avoiding the general point on which the investigation ought to
turn: at another time, they artfully endeavor to interweave their particular interests with the grandeur of Great Britain. They exclaim, that
her commerce with the West Indies, and more than that commerce,
her marine, would, by a suppression of the slave trade, be ruined. This
is very much a matter of doubt: but even if it were not, rather perish
that commerce which derives its existence from the labour of millions
who must pine in a deplorable and hopeless captivity! To every argument that can be advanced us support of such a system, whether drawn
from the interests of trade, or from the difficulty, of even imppssibility
of continuing to cultivate the lands without it, this single answer is
sufficient: It is unjust and inhuman to condemn to perpetual bondage
millions of our fellow-creatures, whose only crime is their happening
to be of a different color from ourselves. But it is for the welfare and
glory of the mother country, that the colonies should flourish: it may

---

* Some of our West Indians are an honour to human nature. But where
a just odium hath, in consequence of a great majority of offenders, fallen
upon any body of people, is not possible, in works of this kind, to point
out each exception.

† The amiable and illustrious *Fenclon* makes the son of *Ulysses* undergo
the hardships of a cruel slavery in the desarts of *Egypt*, in order to render
him compassionate to those whom it was his destiny one day to govern.

be so: but it is more for her glory, and will, ultimately, be more for her advantage too, that the iniquitous Negro trade, odious in the sight of earth and Heaven, should be no more. We cannot prosper, and exist as a great people, while the tears and groans of those afflicted Africans give hourly testimony of our guilt at the throne of the Divinity.

It is insisted, that, without Negroes, there is an end to cultivation. This we may venture to deny. For it hath been observed by many sensible persons, that in much of the work at present done by slaves, (as far, at least, as respects the carrying of burthens) asses might be employed with considerable benefit. The ass is hardly an animal, cheaply purchased, and easily maintained. The less laborious tasks might be performed by hired servants, (Europeans, or manumitted slaves) and by bondmen condemned to slavery for their crimes. Instead of immolating annually at the gallows so many hundreds of robust robbers, remit them to your plantations, to alleviate the toils of your overworked and unoffending Negroes. Should it be objected that those could not support, for any length of time, the climate of the West Indies, when united with labour, would it not then be worthy the wisdom of the Legislature by various inducements to encourage marriages amongst them? One may reasonably suppose, that their offspring, born and bred in the islands, would be as well able to endure the effects of the climate, as the Negro imported from the regions of Africa.

Should encouragement be also given to the population of the Blacks, their children, born in the Caribbee islands, would be likewise more capable of labour than any slaves imported; and as a consequence of freedom, or even of mild usage, they would do more work, and better work, (for they would do it more chearfully,) and would become more attached and faithful to their employers. As their condition improved, they would consume more of the produce and manufactures of Great Britain, to the considerable augmentation of her commerce and revenue. In each island a spacious building might be erected and endowed, for the reception and support of aged and infirm Negroes. Schools also should be established in convenient situations, for introducing the children in reading and writing, and in the principles and practice of the Christian Religion. To ensure the success of such a project, well qualified inspectors should be appointed to make an annual visit.

The laws should oblige the respective proprietors to have, within a year from the passing of the act, one black woman for every Negro on their estates. Let proper inspectors make the circuit of each island, to see that the legal proportion be preserved; every proprietor whose black women shall be unequal in number to his Negroes, to pay a tax of twenty shillings for each woman deficient, towards the fund for the establishment and support of the Seminaries. At the end of the year the inspector may make a second circuit, and such persons as shall have complied with the law, and compleated their proportion of women, may be exonerated from the tax, on receiving his certificate.

But the most eligible plan for the planter to pursue, would be to give his Negroes a sort of interest in their occupation. By the custom of permitting them to purchase out their freedom, which prevails in the Spanish colonies, the proprietor would be reimbursed the original cost of them. Emancipate your slaves – allow them wages – gratify the most deserving with offices about your plantations – contrive to reward them with even an imaginary degree of consequence, and see whether the same portion of labour could not be executed by half the number you, at present, employ. Work performed under terrour of the scourage, never was, nor ever will be, equal, either in the quantity or excellence, to that of hired labourers.

To what is the superior prosperity of the French islands attributed? To the superior wisdom, and to the humanity of the planters, in the regulation of their slaves*. This management is partly owing to the mildness if their own manners, and partly to the nature of their government, which is arbitrary. That arbitrary power should ever be a friend to liberty, or to the alleviation of slavery, may appear a thing too opposite to its very nature to be admitted. But so it is; and that so it hath been; the history of Rome is an evidence. The known story of Augustus and Vedius Pollio † is sufficient to support the assertion. An individual in the French islands dares not be tyrannical: he is kept in awe by a higher and stronger hand, that would instantly crush him, should avaricious views of private emolument tempt him to dishonor or endammage the community. I am not panegyrizing absolute government: - God forbid! – but even in the world of governments, even in despotism, may something be displayed, not unworthy of the respect and imitation of a free people.

---

* See Smith's Wealth of Nations, Vol. II. p. 394 and 395.

† Who, while the emperor was at supper with him, ordered a slave to be hewn in pieces and thrown into a fish-pond, for breaking an ewer. Augustus commanded him to liberate all his slaves *immediately*.

The French planter resides on his estate. His slaves are not abandoned to an agent. One acre in ten is planted for the support of the Negroes. Thus they depend not on imported provisions; while the slave, who is attached to the soil, acquires some interest in what he is suffered to possess, which terminates in the profit and security of the proprietor.

Distinct employments should be assigned. The slave that hath wrought all day at the sugar-canes, should not be goaded in the evening to a new and oppressive labour.

But further. – The object of the Legislature will, doubtless, be, either wholly to abolish the Negro trade, or to promote its gradual dissolution. Should the former plan take place, let us confider its consequences. The amount of the Blacks in our part of the West Indies is nearly 420,000. The annual importation from Africa is stated to be about 100,000. Thirty thousand, at the least, of these are destined for the market of the British islands. The proportion, then, between the number annually imported, and the Negroes already in the colonies, is as one to fourteen. But it is usual to allow for a loss of one fifth of each cargo, by mortality at sea, and of one third in the seasoning afterwards on shore. Now, deducting the numbers which perish in the seasoning, and taking into the account of the loss of labour incurred before the survivors are fit for plantation business, the proportion will be reduced still further, and we shall find the mischief of a total abolition would be nothing like so severe, as it is at present apprehended; even on the supposition that the deficiency of labour could not be supplied from other sources. But supplied it might be, there is every reason to believe, from Europe and America, by offering such wages, backed by judicious bounties, and strengthened by favourable regulations, as would induce very many to go over to the British colonies. Thus the deficiency occasioned by suppressing the annual market would be found inconsiderable, and might be easily remedied by hired labourers. For suppose that 21,000 slaves of the annual importation (which is in the proportion of one to twenty, between them and the gross number), after all due destruction hath been made, remain to be divided amongst the British islands. These, at 60l. a man, would cost 1,260,000l. (Observe that, for the first year, their labour is unproductive.) Now, the annual produce of the islands is said to be five millions. The total loss, therefore, to the whole body of planters could not exceed 250,000l. that is, the one twentieth part of their annual produce, and consequently would be equivalent to no more than a land-tax of one shilling in the pound. The maintenance, cloathing, and other necessaries, for these 21,000 slaves, would, at the rate of 3l. *per annum**, each man, amount to 63,000l. Therefore, altho' we cannot accurately say what the expence would be of a number of hired servants, sufficient to fill the void made by non-importation, we may yet safely pronounce that it would not amount to more (perhaps not even to as much) than hath been stated as the annual expenditure for slaves. With this must be considered the losses sustained from the sickness of slaves, and from deaths occasioned by barbarity; the latter of which could not happen to free servants, the former less frequently than to the half-starved and ill-clad Negroes.

	£
*	
21,000 slaves, at 60l. per head, will cost	1,260,000
Their annual maintenance, at 3l. per head	63,000
Total expence for one year	1,323,000
Let us say, for argument's sake,	
21,000 hired labourers, at 10l. bounty each man,	210,000
Expence of passage, maintenance, and wages for	
one year, at 30l. per man,	630,000
Total annual expence	840,000
Total expence of 21,000 slaves for one year	1,323,000
Ditto for 21,000 hired servants	840,000
Balance in favour of the planters	483,000

Even allowing the expence of a hired labourer to be 50l. per annum, bounty included, there would still be a balance in favour of the planters. For, 21,000 hired labourers, at 50l. per man, would amount to 1,050,000l. this sum deducted from 1,323,000l. leaves a balance of 273,000l.

	£
	1,323,000
	1,050,000

	273,000

The heavy loss occasioned by such slaves as die in the seasoning, which amount to about one third, is not to be forgotten.

The numbers of Europeans employed by the East Indian Company, in a climate as hot and unwholesome as that of the Caribbee islands, is an ample proof that white labourers could execute the work in the West Indies, as well as Africans; especially now, that the climate is improved. White men were the first cultivators of sugar. Mean while, the Blacks already in the islands would, in consequence of an act for their better treatment, (if not for their infranchisement) by means of wholesome and sufficient nourishment, and of justly proportioning their labour to their powers, increase considerably in population; provided that a proper supply of women were imported for a few years, until every Negro should have one woman: and to this the planters should be obliged by law.

But should the measure of an immediate prohibition be rejected, might not the gradual extinction of the slave trade be thus accomplished? Let it be strictly confined to our own colonies, and the number of limited to their present wants, with such a proportion of women as would advance population. * Each ship should, in order to prevent a mortality, be obliged to proportion her cargo to her tonnage, and her crew to her cargo. For at present a vessel of but 100 tons burthen will take in 250 Negroes, who, for want of sufficient room, are linked together in a most afflicting situation, and, by reason of the scanty

---

* Let us state in thus. – British subjects may trade for slaves to the coast of Africa only, in vessels of not less than 500 tons burthen, upon giving security that they will vend their slaves in the British West Indies, and not elsewhere. No slaves to be re-exported from any part of his Majesty's dominions.
Only thirty thousand Negroes to be imported into the islands, the first year after the passing of the act.
    22,500, in the next year.
    18,000, in the next.
    12,000, in the next.
     8,000, in the next.
     4,000, in the next; and then the slave trade to cease entirely. –
Each ship to have a license from the Commissioners of the Customs, in which shall be specified the name of the owner, the ship, the master and mate, and the tonnage of the vessel.
No ship to carry more than one slave for each ton, on pain of forfeiture of [*illegible*]. The owner to enter into a recognizance to comply with the directions of the act.

complement of seamen, are treated with double rigour to prevent insurrection. This rule for proportioning the crews, together with proper regulations for the comfortable accommodation and victualing of the Blacks while on board, would, by lessening the profits of the trade, tend insensibly to a total abolition. Importations then being once discontinued, it would behove the planters to cherish to the utmost the slaves remaining in the islands, and to encourage their increase. It is the expectation of replacing them from the African ships that, in a great measure, induces masters who are blind to their true interest, and deaf to the voice of compassion, to perpetrate such wanton and unutterable cruelties. – The laws might afterwards, from time to time, promote manumission, till at length a general emancipation should take place.

The improvements, proposed might, doubtless, at the beginning meet with some obstructions. But perseverance, and, most of all, a hearty desire to favour their progress and facilitate their execution, would bear down every difficulty. Should the profits of the planter suffer even a temporary diminution, (and that they would is by no means clear) he must be recompensed in the end, by a measure that would at once advance the interests of individuals, and the virtue, force and dignity of the nation. Neither private nor publick opulence can be maintained by iniquity. /there is but this alternative for the planters; either to persist in their present oppressive system, and draw down vengeance on themselves and their fellow subjects, or consent to and encourage a reformation, and, by establishing our grandeur on a more firm base, secure the future glory and advantage of the British people.

Should they oppose, however, these humane propositions, it will then be the duty of the Legislature to shut its eyes against the interests of intractable individuals, and to act for the empire at large. Should the obstinacy of the planters occasion such a crisis, it might be no improper question for debate, whether we should not abandon their sugars all together. "We could purchase them cheaper from other countries: the foreign islands undersell ours, and the competition to supply us would probably prevent the price from being raised."* This step, although it would diminish the wealth of some luxurious proprietors, would neither ruin or marine, our manufacturers, nor our revenue. For the loss to our marine could be amply compensated by the trade we relinquished for the West India monopoly, and by turning a more

* Lord Sheffield's Observations on the Commerce of the American States, p. 188.

vigorous attention to the fisheries. The latter alone, if pursued, with the full energy that an object so important and inestimable requires, would provide us not only with vast augmentation at once to our shipping, our seamen, and our commerce, but would also, by condensing the national force, create a solidity and compactness of power, that must continue us a formidable and triumphant people. The fisheries are an innocent source of riches: no slave bleeds under the lash of a cruel overseer to procure us that fund of opulence. The disadvantage with respect to the vent for our manufacturers might be remedied by the European branches of commerce, which afford us a market less remote for our commodities, and quicker and more certain returns. The wealth of Britain hath not increased in the same proportion as that of the colonies: for though she hath engrossed the whole of their foreign trade, she hath been withdrawing her capitals from other channels, in order to employ them in her commerce in the West Indies.* Now, that branch of commerce which hath been suffered to decay in compliment to the colony trade, would, we may naturally suppose, revive and be re-invigorated, were that with the plantations to be diminished or destroyed: it would rise again upon the ruins of the latter, and console us for the dereliction. Advantages in revenue would succeed of course: the expense of defending the islands overbalances the benefits we derive from their revenue. If sugar then be the grand article in which slaves are employed, and the remaining products can be cultivated by freemen – if sugars can be produced at a cheaper rate from other nations – if the loss to our marine could be more than indemnified, by the fisheries at home, and by the foreign trade restored to us on our relinquishing the colonies – if our manufactures could be furnished with a market nearer home, and could therefore obtain returns more rapid and more sure – if the charge of protecting the West India plantations devours the revenue arising from their advantages, and if the balance of the trade be a million and a half against us, will it be consistent with the good sense, the true interest, and the majesty of this kingdom, to hesitate on a measure which cannot cause the mischief that the planters pretend, of this kingdom, to hesitate on a measure which cannot cause the mischief that the planters pretend, and will ultimately insure the wealth and honour of our empire?

Incontrovertible as the maxim is, it is yet no easy matter to convince a commercial people, that that greatness which is grounded on a

* Smith's Wealth of Nations, Vol. II. p. 410.

violation of the freedom and happiness of other nations, is a treacherous prosperity, and must terminate, ere long, in its own humiliation. The shallow politician, and the craving monopolist, smile at the idea of a Supreme Being interfering in the splendor or decline of empires. It is the first duty of a Legislature to watch over the virtue of the people it directs: but the Legislature of a state that is aggrandized by commerce may sometimes, by the selfish importunity of merchants, be led inconsiderately to betray its trust, and unawares promote iniquity.

Let us now, in a few words, re-examine, and turn into common English the arguments already noted in support of the slave trade.

Firstly. – Acts of parliament have countenanced this commerce, and permitted that Negroes should be a species of traffic, should be as elephants, teeth, wax, and leather, should be as chattels, assets, hereditaments, &c.* - and therefore the slave trade is just and laudable.

2dly. – Numbers of the poor in England are (it is insisted) in as wretched condition as the Negroes in the plantations † - therefore is the slave trade just and laudable.

3dly. – Our miners (who are freemen, and well paid for their labour) lead as miserable lives as the slaves in the West Indies ‡ - therefore slave trade is, &c.

4thly. – The British Legislature admits of slavery (that is, a temporary restraint of liberty for the defence of the realm) in the impressing of seamen § - therefore, &c.

5thly. – The Blacks are a naughty and unpolished people ¶ - and therefore (although nothing hath been done for their civilization) the slave trade, &c.

6thly. – Their noses are flat, and their skins not white; from which we have the very best reason to infer that the Almighty intended them to for slaves from the beginning ** - therefore is the Negro trade, &c.

7thly. – Their intellects are dull†† (a point disputed; nay, an assertion well refuted) – therefore, &c.

---

* Considerations on the Negro Cause of Somerset and Knowles.

† Apology for Negro Slavery, or the West India Planter vindicated.

‡ Idem.

§ Considerations, &c.

¶ Apology, &c.

** Considerations, &c.

†† Idem.

8thly. – If we abolish the barbarous system in our colonies, the welfare of Britain would be injured, that is, a few planters of overgrown fortunes would be likely (perhaps) to lose some of their emoluments – and therefore (although the Author of all Good hates injustice and cruelty, and sooner or later sense destruction on a guilty nation) the Negro slave trade is just and laudable.

9thly. – The Europeans in the colonies could not so ingenious-ly regulate and govern (that is, domineer, and gratify their imperious dispositions) over free white men, as over the captive and dispirited Negroes – and therefore, &c.

10thly. – When the Blacks are unshipped in the islands, they are delighted to meet with their friends and acquaintances. * They have a dance in the evening – and therefore, &c.

To strengthen this reasoning, they remind us of the moral sense – links of creation – and Mr. Locke; - abuse Mr. Hargrave and the Earl of Mansfield † - sneer at Aristotle and Moses, the Quakers and the Clergy. One of them ‡ affects to decide the affair by dint of definition. "Slavery, my Lord," says he, "is that state of subjection which mankind by force, or other wise, is a term of immense circumference, and may contain every crime of which human nature is capable. The acquiring a state of subjection, is also worthy of some notice. A nation may fall into, and suffer, but I never before heard of one acquiring a state of subjection, whatever it might chance to do with a state of superiority. But the question at present before the publick is, not what is slavery, but (be it what it may) whether it ought, or ought not to be abolished; and, if not, whether it should undergo such a modification, as would render it tolerable to the slave, advantageous to the planter, and neither inglo-rious nor unprofitable to the community. We are not debating about force or otherwise, but are considering whether it be not injustice and villainy, in the highest degree, to subject many millions of the human race to the rigours of a lawless and infamous domination.

What are the petty interests of any set of men, what is this deceit-ful opulence of the empire, to the delivery of millions from unmerited oppression? The world is every day becoming more enlightened. As a consequence of improvement in civilization, the hardships of villeinage were abolished in England. From our further progress in refinement,

* Apology, p. 22.
† Considerations, &c.
‡ Idem.

there is reason to hope that those laws will be obliterated which countenance the slave trade. A spirit of indulgence, in the home department, distinguishes the present times. Parliament hath acknowledged
the absurdity and oppression of the popery laws, and relaxed their
rigour. Parliament hath been merciful to the children of those men
whose estates were confiscated for the Scottish rebellion. It casts an eye
of pity, form period to period, on the prison of the helpless debtor, and
restores him from anguish to the blessings of liberty. Let some portion
therefore of this national beneficence be extended beyond the limits
of our European possessions, and the native of Africa, groaning in the
West Indies, be an object of commiseration to the Senate of Great Britain. Let not her wealth and power be extracted from blood and misery.
Her commerce is the pillar of her glory; if it be founded on iniquity, it
must give way. It is idle to imagine that slaves could be obtained clan-
destinely from other nations concerned in this traffic. Double prices,
double losses, double danger, and tenfold bribery through all our har-
bours in the West Indies, would accumulate an expence that no planter
could supply. Nay more: should this detestable source of gain be discontinued in this kingdom, our neighbours on the continent will soon
follow the example. They will be ashamed to pursue the trade, when
the principles of our conduct are proclaimed from pole to pole: they
will be afraid to pursue it, lest the slaves in their own colonies, jealous
of the enjoyments of their countrymen in ours, should sigh for the
same comforts, and dissatisfaction, fury, and revolt, spread desolation
through America. Yes, let Britain shew the way; the same elevated ideas
of legislation and policy will be rapidly adopted by the rest of Europe:
the happy contagion will extend to every realm, whenever the displays
of the signal of emancipation. Superior in arts, in arms, in commerce,
let her assume a pre-eminence in Justice and Humanity. To be the first
in doing good is a godlike supremacy. Should this event take place,
what a harvest of triumph from a deed so sublime, and so worthy of the
fame and majesty of the British people! But if neither the iniquitious
nature of the trade itself – nor its alarming effects in the destruction
of our seamen – nor the fraud, the oppression, the carnage it occasions through the numerous and extensive regions of one quarter of the
globe – nor the cruelties inflicted on those fettered Africans in a long,
and often distressful voyage – nor the painful and lasting servitude
they are destined to endure – nor their tears and groans, their stripes,
their tortures, their shocking executions, can prevail with our Legisla-

ture, either to mitigate their sufferings, or snatch them at once from those atrocious barbarians who are sullying unrebuked the renown of / british equity, and blasting the glory of a splendid and mighty nation, at least let this awful reflection have some weight, let us consider that, although the divine vengeance hath not yet overwhelmed us, the wrath of the Omnipotent will not sleep for ever. FINIS.

Thoughts and Sentiments on the Evil of Slavery

Thoughts and Sentiments on the Evil and Wicked Traffic of the Slavery and Commerce of the Human Species, Humbly Submitted to the Inhabitants of Great-Britan By Ottobah Cugoano, A Native of Africa.

He that stealeth a man and selleth him, or maketh merchandize of him, or if he be founds in his hand: than that thief shall die.

LAW OF GOD.

LONDON:
PRINTED IN THE YEAR
M.DCC.LXXXVII.

Thoughts and Sentiments on the Evil of Slavery

One law, and one manner shall be for you, and for the stranger that sojourneth with you; and therefore, all things whatsoever ye would that men should do to you, do ye even so to them.

Numb. xv.16.—Math. vii.12.

As several learned gentlemen of distinguished abilities, as well as eminent for their great humanity, liberality and candour, have written various essays against that infamous traffic of the African Slave Trade, carried on with the West-India planters and merchants, to the great shame and disgrace of all Christian nations wherever it is admitted in any of their territories, or in any place or situation amongst them; it cannot be amiss that I should thankfully acknowledge these truly worthy and humane gentlemen with the warmest sense of gratitude, for their beneficent and laudable endeavours towards a total suppression of that infamous and iniquitous traffic of stealing, kid-napping, buying, selling, and cruelly enslaving men!

Those who have endeavoured to restore to their fellow-creatures the common rights of nature, of which especially the poor unfortunate Black People have been so unjustly deprived, cannot fail in meeting with the applause of all good men, and the approbation of that which will for ever redound to their honor; they have the warrant of that which is divine: *Open thy mouth, judge righteously, plead the cause of the poor and needy; for the liberal deviseth liberal things, and by liberal things shall stand.* And they can say with the pious Job, *Did not I weep for him that was in trouble; was not my soul grieved for the poor?*

The kind exertions of many benevolent and humane gentlemen, against the iniquitous traffic of slavery and oppression, has been attended with much good to many, and must redound with great honor to themselves, to humanity and their country; their laudable endeavours have been productive of the most beneficent effects in preventing that savage barbarity from taking place in free countries at home. In this, as well as in many other respects, there is one class of people (whose virtues of probity and humanity are well known) who are worthy of universal approbation and imitation, because, like men of hon-

53

or and humanity, they have jointly agreed to carry on no slavery and savage barbarity among them; and, since the last war, some mitigation of slavery has been obtained in some respective districts of America, though not in proportion to their own vaunted claims of freedom; but it is to be hoped, that they will yet go on to make a further and greater reformation. However, notwithstanding all that has been done and written against it, that brutish barbarity, and unparalelled injustice, is still carried on to a very great extent in the colonies, and with an avidity as insidious, cruel and oppressive as ever. The longer that men continue in the practice of evil and wickedness, they grow the more abandoned; for nothing in history can equal the barbarity and cruelty of the tortures and murders committed under various pretences in modern slavery, except the annals of the Inquisition and the bloody edicts of Popish massacres.

It is therefore manifest, that something else ought yet to be done; and what is required, is evidently the incumbent duty of all men of enlightened understanding, and of every man that has any claim or affinity to the name of Christian, that the base treatment which the African Slaves undergo, ought to be abolished; and it is moreover evident, that the whole, or any part of that iniquitous traffic of slavery, can no where, or in any degree, be admitted, but among those who must eventually resign their own claim to any degree of sensibility and humanity, for that of barbarians and russians.

But it would be needless to arrange an history of all the base treatment which the African Slaves are subjected to, in order to shew the exceeding wickedness and evil of that insidious traffic, as the whole may easily appear in every part, and at every view, to be wholly and totally inimical to every idea of justice, equity, reason and humanity. What I intend to advance against that evil, criminal and wicked traffic of enslaving men, are only some Thoughts and Sentiments which occur to me, as being obvious from the Scriptures of Divine Truth, or such arguments as are chiefly deduced from thence, with other such observations as I have been able to collect. Some of these observations may lead into a larger field of consideration, than that of the African Slave Trade alone; but those causes from wherever they originate, and become the production of slavery, the evil effects produced by it, must shew that its origin and source is of a wicked and criminal nature.

No necessity, or any situation of men, however poor, pitiful and wretched they may be, can warrant them to rob others, or oblige them to become thieves, because they are poor, miserable and wretched: But the robbers of men, the kidnappers, ensnarers and slave-holders, who take away the common rights and privileges of others to support and enrich themselves, are universally those pitiful and detestable wretches; for the ensnaring of others, and taking away their liberty by slavery and oppression, is the worst kind of robbery, as most opposite to every precept and injunction of the Divine Law, and contrary to that command which enjoins that *all men should love their neighbours as themselves, and that they should do unto others, as they would that men should do to them.* As to any other laws that slave-holders may make among themselves, as respecting slaves, they can be of no better kind, nor give them any better character, than what is implied in the common report—that there may be some honesty among thieves. This may seem a harsh comparison, but the parallel is so coincident that, I must say, I can find no other way of expressing my Thoughts and Sentiments, without making use of some harsh words and comparisons against the carriers on of such abandoned wickedness. But, in this little undertaking, I must humbly hope the impartial reader will excuse such defects as may arise from want of better education; and as to the resentment of those who can lay their cruel lash upon the backs of thousands, for a thousand times less crimes than writing against their enormous wickedness and brutal avarice, is what I may be sure to meet with.

However, it cannot but be very discouraging to a man of my complexion in such an attempt as this, to meet with the evil aspersions of some men, who say, "That an African is not entitled to any competent degree of knowledge, or capable of imbibing any sentiments of probity; and that nature designed him for some inferior link in the chain, fitted only to be a slave."

But when I meet with those who make no scruple to deal with the human species, as with the beasts of the earth, I must think them not only brutish, but wicked and base; and that their aspersions are insidious and false: And if such men can boast of greater degrees of knowledge, than any African is entitled to, I shall let them enjoy all the advantages of it unenvied, as I fear it consists only in a greater share of infidelity, and that of a blacker kind than only skin deep. And if their complexion be not what I may suppose, it is at least the nearest in resemblance to an infernal hue. A good man will neither speak nor do as a bad man will; but if a man is bad it makes no difference whether he be a black or a white devil.

By some of such complexion, as whether black or white it matters not, I was early snatched away from my native country, with about eighteen or twenty more boys and girls, as we were playing in a field. We lived but a few days journey from the coast where we were kidnapped, and as we were decoyed and drove along, we were soon conducted to a factory, and from thence, in the fashionable way of traffic, consigned to Grenada. Perhaps it may not be amiss to give a few remarks, as some account of myself, on this transposition of captivity.

I was born in the city of Agimaque, on the coast of Fantyn; my father was a companion to the chief in that part of the country of Fantee, and when the old king died I was left in his house with his family; soon after I was sent for by his nephew, Ambro Accasa, who succeeded the old king in the chiefdom of that part of Fantee known by the name of Agimaque and Assinee. I lived with his children, enjoying peace and tranquillity, about twenty moons, which, according to their way of reckoning time, is two years. I was sent for to visit an uncle, who lived at a considerable distance from Agimaque. The first day after we set out we arrived at Assinee, and the third day at my uncle's habitation, where I lived about three months, and was then thinking of returning to my father and young companion at Agimaque; but by this time I had got well acquainted with some of the children of my uncle's hundreds of relations, and we were some days too ventursome in going into the woods to gather fruit and catch birds, and such amusements as pleased us. One day I refused to go with the rest, being rather apprehensive that something might happen to us; till one of my play-fellows said to me, because you belong to the great men, you are afraid to venture your carcase, or else of the bounsam, which is the devil. This enraged me so much, that I set a resolution to join the rest, and we went into the woods as usual; but we had not been above two hours before our troubles began, when several great ruffians came upon us suddenly, and said we had committed a fault against their lord, and we must go and answer for it ourselves before him.

Some of us attempted in vain to run away, but pistols and cutlasses were soon introduced, threatening, that if we offered to stir we should all lie dead on the spot. One of them pretended to be more friendly than the rest, and said, that he would speak to their lord to get us clear, and desired that we should follow him; we were then immediately divided into different parties, and drove after him. We were soon led out of the way which we knew, and towards the evening, as we came in sight of a town, they told us that this great man of theirs lived there, but pretended it was too late to go and see him that night. Next morning there came three other men, whose language differed from ours, and spoke to some of those who watched us all the night, but he that pretended to be our friend with the great man, and some others, were gone away. We asked our keepers what these men had been saying to them, and they answered, that they had been asking them, and us together, to go and feast with them that day, and that we must put off seeing the great man till after; little thinking that our doom was so nigh, or that these villains meant to feast on us as their prey. We went with them again about half a day's journey, and came to a great multitude of people, having different music playing; and all the day after we got there, we were very merry with the music, dancing and singing. Towards the evening, we were again persuaded that we could not get back to where the great man lived till next day; and when bedtime came, we were separated into different houses with different people. When the next morning came, I asked for the men that brought me there, and for the rest of my companions; and I was told that they were gone to the sea side to bring home some rum, guns and powder, and that some of my companions were gone with them, and that some were gone to the fields to do something or other. This gave me strong suspicion that there was some treachery in the case, and I began to think that my hopes of returning home again were all over. I soon became very uneasy, not knowing what to do, and refused to eat or drink for whole days together, till the man of the house told me that he would do all in his power to get me back to my uncle; then I eat a little fruit with him, and had some thoughts that I should be sought after, as I would be then missing at home about five or six days. I enquired every day if the men had come back, and for the rest of my companions, but could get no answer of any satisfaction. I was kept about six days at this man's house, and in the evening there was another man came and talked with him a good while, and I heard the one say to the other he must go, and the other said the sooner the better; that man came out and told me that he knew my relations at Agimaque, and that we must set out to-morrow morning, and he would convey me there. Accordingly we set out next day, and travelled till dark, when we came to a place where we had some supper and slept. He carried a large bag with some gold dust, which he said he had to buy some goods at the sea side to take with him to Agimaque. Next day we travelled on, and in the evening came to a town, where I saw several white people, which made me afraid that they would eat me, according to our notion as children in the inland parts of the country. This made me rest very uneasy all the night, and next morning I had some victuals brought, desiring me to eat and make haste, as my guide and kid-napper told me that he had to go to the castle with some company that were going there, as he had told me before, to get some goods. After I was ordered out, the horrors I soon saw and felt, cannot be well described; I saw many of my miserable countrymen chained two and two, some hand-cuffed, and some with their hands tied behind. We were conducted along by a guard, and when we arrived at the castle, I asked my guide what I was brought there for, he told me to learn the ways of the browfow, that is the white faced people. I saw him take a gun, a piece of cloth, and some lead for me, and then he told me that he must now leave me there, and went off. This made me cry bitterly, but I was soon conducted to a prison, for three days, where I heard the groans and cries of many, and saw some of my fellow-captives. But when a vessel arrived to conduct us away to the ship, it was a most horrible scene; there was nothing to be heard but rattling of chains, smacking of whips, and the groans and cries of our fellow-men. Some would not stir from the ground, when they were lashed and beat in the most horrible manner. I have forgot the name of this infernal fort; but we were taken in the ship that came for us, to another that was ready to sail from Cape Coast. When we were put into the ship, we saw several black merchants coming on board, but we were all drove into our holes, and not suffered to speak to any of them. In this situation we continued several days in sight of our native land; but I could find no good person to give any information of my situation to Accasa at Agimaque. And when we found ourselves at last taken away, death was more preferable than life, and a plan was concerted amongst us, that we might burn and blow up the ship, and to perish all together in the flames; but we were betrayed by one of our own countrywomen, who slept with some of the head men of the ship, for it was common for the dirty filthy sailors to take the African women and lie upon their bodies; but the men were chained and pent up in holes. It was the women and boys which were to burn the ship, with the approbation and groans of the rest; though that was prevented, the discovery was likewise a cruel bloody scene.

But it would be needless to give a description of all the horrible scenes which we saw, and the base treatment which we met with in this dreadful captive situation, as the similar cases of thousands, which suffer by this infernal traffic, are well known. Let it suffice to say, that I was thus lost to my dear indulgent parents and relations, and they to me. All my help was cries and tears, and these could not avail; nor suffered long, till one succeeding woe, and dread, swelled up another. Brought from a state of innocence and freedom, and, in a barbarous and cruel manner, conveyed to a state of horror and slavery: This abandoned situation may be easier conceived than described. From the time that I was kid-napped and conducted to a factory, and from thence in the brutish, base, but fashionable way of traffic, consigned to Grenada, the grievous thoughts which I then felt, still pant in my heart; though my fears and tears have long since subsided. And yet it is still grievous to think that thousands more have suffered in similar and greater distress, under the hands of barbarous robbers, and merciless taskmasters; and that many even now are suffering in all the extreme bitterness of grief and woe, that no language can describe The cries of some, and the sight of their misery, may be seen and heard afar; but the deep sounding groans of thousands, and the great sadness of their misery and woe, under the heavy load of oppressions and calamities inflicted upon them, are such as can only be distinctly known to the ears of Jehovah Sabaoth.

This Lord of Hosts, in his great Providence, and in great mercy to me, made a way for my deliverance from Grenada.—Being in this dreadful captivity and horrible slavery, without any hope of deliverance, for about eight or nine months, beholding the most dreadful scenes of misery and cruelty, and seeing my miserable companions often cruelly lashed, and as it were cut to pieces, for the most trifling faults; this made me often tremble and weep, but I escaped better than many of them. For eating a piece of sugarcane, some were cruelly lashed, or struck over the face to knock their teeth out. Some of the stouter ones, I suppose often reproved, and grown hardened and stupid with many cruel beatings and lashings, or perhaps faint and pressed with hunger and hard labour, were often committing trespasses of this kind, and when detected, they met with exemplary punishment. Some told me they had their teeth pulled out to deter others, and to prevent them from eating any cane in future. Thus seeing my miserable companions and countrymen in this pitiful, distressed and horrible situation, with all the brutish baseness and barbarity attending it, could not but fill my little mind with horror and indignation. But I must own, to the shame of my own countrymen, that I was first kid-napped and betrayed by some of my own complexion, who were the first cause of my exile and slavery; but if there were no buyers there would be no sellers. So far as I can remember, some of the Africans in my country keep slaves, which they take in war, or for debt; but those which they keep are well fed, and good care taken of them, and treated well; and, as to their cloathing, they differ according to the custom of the country. But I may safely say, that all the poverty and misery that any of the inhabitants of Africa meet with among themselves, is far inferior to those inhospitable regions of misery which they meet with in the West-Indies, where their hard-hearted overseers have neither regard to the laws of God, nor the life of their fellow-men.

Thanks be to God, I was delivered from Grenada, and that horrid brutal slavery.—A gentleman coming to England, took me for his servant, and brought me away, where I soon found my situation become more agreeable. After coming to England, and seeing others write and read, I had a strong desire to learn, and getting what assistance I could, I applied myself to learn reading and writing, which soon became my recreation, pleasure, and delight; and when my master perceived that I could write some, he sent me to a proper school for that purpose to learn. Since, I have endeavoured to improve my mind in reading, and have sought to get all the intelligence I could, in my situation of life, towards the state of my brethren and countrymen in complexion, and of the miserable situation of those who are barbarously sold into captivity, and unlawfully held in slavery.

But, among other observations, one great duty I owe to Almighty God, (the thankful acknowledgement I would not omit for any consideration) that, although I have been brought away from my native country, in that torrent of robbery and wickedness, thanks be to God for his good providence towards me; I have both obtained liberty, and acquired the great advantages of some little learning, in being able to read and write, and, what is still infinitely of greater advantage, I trust, to know something of HIM *who is that God whose providence rules over all, and who is the only Potent One that rules in the nations over the children of men. It is unto Him, who is the Prince of the Kings of the earth, that I would give all thanks.* And, in some manner, I may say with Joseph, as he did with respect to the evil intention of his brethren, when they sold him into Egypt, that whatever evil intentions and bad motives those insidious robbers had in carrying me away from my native country and friends, I trust, was what the Lord intended for my good. In this respect, I am highly indebted to many of the good people of England for learning and principles unknown to the people of my native country. But, above all, what have I obtained from the Lord God of Hosts, the God of the Christians! in that divine revelation of the only true God, and the Saviour of men, what a treasure of wisdom and blessings are involved? How wonderful is the divine goodness displayed in those invaluable books the Old and New Testaments, that inestimable compilation of books, the Bible? And, O what a treasure to have, and one of the greatest advantages to be able to read therein, and a divine blessing to understand *!

But, to return to my subject, I begin with the Cursory Remarker. This man stiles himself a friend to the West-India colonies and their inhabitants, like Demetrius, the silversmith, a man of some considerable abilities, seeing their craft in danger, a craft, however, not so innocent and justifiable as the making of shrines for Diana, though that was base and wicked enough to enslave the minds of men with superstition and idolatry; but his craft, and the gain of those craftsmen, consists in the enslaving both soul and body to the cruel idolatry, and most abominable service and slavery, to the idol of cursed avarice: And as he finds some discoveries of their wicked traffic held up in a light where truth and facts are so clearly seen, as none but the most desperate villain would dare to obstruct or oppose, he therefore sallies forth with all the

* The justly celebrated Dr. Young, in recommending this divine book of heavenly wisdom to the giddy and thoughtless world, in his Night Thoughts, has the following elegant lines:

> Perhaps thou'dst langh but at thine own expence,
> This counsel strange should I presume to give;
> Retire and read thy Bible to be gay;
> There truths abound of sov'reign aid to peace.
> Ah, do not prize it less because inspired.
> Read and revere the sacred page; a page,
> Where triumphs immortality; a page,
> Which not the whole creation could produce;
> Which not the conflagration shall destroy;
> In nature's ruin not one letter's lost,
> 'Tis printed in the mind of gods for ever,
> Angels and men assent to what I sing!

desperation of an Utopian assailant, to tell lies by a virulent contradiction of facts, and with false aspersions endeavour to calumniate the worthy and judicious essayest of that discovery, a man, whose character is irreproachable. By thus artfully supposing, if he could bring the reputation of the author, who has discovered so much of their iniquitous traffic, into dispute, his work would fall and be less regarded. However, this virulent craftsman has done no great merit to his cause and the credit of that infamous craft; at the appearance of truth, his understanding has got the better of his avarice and infidelity, so far, as to draw the following concession: "I shall not be so far misunderstood, by the candid and judicious part of mankind, as to be ranked among the advocates of slavery, as I most sincerely join Mr. Ramsay *, and every other man of sensibility, in hoping the blessings of freedom will, in due time, be equally diffused over the whole globe."

By this, it would seem that he was a little ashamed of his craftsmen, and would not like to be ranked or appear amongst them. But as long as there are any hopes of gain to be made by that insidious craft, he can join with them well enough, and endeavour to justify them in that most abandoned traffic of buying, selling, and enslaving men. He finds fault with a plan for punishing robbers, thieves and vagabonds, who distress their neighbours by their thrift, robbery and plunder, without regarding any laws human or divine, except the rules of their own fraternity, and in that case, according to the proverb, there may be some honor among thieves; but these are the only people in the world that ought to suffer some punishment, imprisonment or slavery; their external complexion, whether black or white, should be no excuse for them to do evil. Being aware of this, perhaps he was afraid that some of his friends, the great and opulent banditti of slave-holders in the western part of the world, might be found guilty of more atrocious and complicated crimes, than even those of the highwaymen, the robberies and the petty larcenies committed in England. Therefore, to make the best of this sad dilemma, he brings in a ludicrous invective comparison that it would be "an event which would undoubtedly furnish a new and pleasant compartment to that well known and most delectable print, call'd, The world turn'd up side down, in which the cook is roasted by the pig, the man saddled by the horse," &c. If he means that the complicated banditties of pirates, thieves, robbers, oppressors

---

* The worthy and judicious author of "An Essay on the Treatment and Conversion of the African Slaves in the British Sugar Colonies."

and enslavers of men, are those cooks and men that would be roasted and saddled, it certainly would be no unpleasant sight to see them well roasted, saddled and bridled too; and no matter by whom, whether he terms them pigs, horses or asses. But there is not much likelihood of this silly monkeyish comparison as yet being verified, in bringing the opulent pirates and thieves to condign punishment, so that he could very well bring it in to turn it off with a grin. However, to make use of his words, it would be a most delectable sight, when thieves and robbers get the upper side of the world, to see them turned down; and I should not interrupt his mirth, to see him laugh at his own invective monkeyish comparison as long as he pleases.

But again, when he draws a comparison of the many hardships that the poor in Great-Britain and Ireland labour under, as well as many of those in other countries; that their various distresses are worse than the West India slaves—It may be true, in part, that some of them suffer greater hardships than many of the slaves; but, bad as it is, the poorest in England would not change their situation for that of slaves. And there may be some masters, under various circumstances, worse off than their servants; but they would not change their own situation for theirs: Nor as little would a rich man wish to change his situation of affluence, for that of a beggar: and so, likewise, no freeman, however poor and distressing his situation may be, would resign his liberty for that of a slave, in the situation of a horse or a dog. The case of the poor, whatever their hardships may be, in free countries, is widely different from that of the West-India slaves. For the slaves, like animals, are bought and sold, and dealt with as their capricious owners may think fit, even in torturing and tearing them to pieces, and wearing them out with hard labour, hunger and oppression; and should the death of a slave ensue by some other more violent way than that which is commonly the death of thousands, and tens of thousands in the end, the haughty tyrant, in that case, has only to pay a small fine for the murder and death of his slave. The brute creation in general may fare better than man, and some dogs may refuse the crumbs that the distressed poor would be glad of; but the nature and situation of man is far superior to that of beasts; and, in like manner, whatever circumstances poor freemen may be in, their situation is much superior, beyond any proportion, to that of the hardships and cruelty of modern slavery. But where can the situation of any freeman be so bad as that of a slave; or, could such be found, or even worse, as he would have it, what would the comparison amount to? Would it plead for his craft of slavery and oppression? Or, rather, would it not cry aloud for some redress, and what every well regulated society of men ought to hear and consider, that none should suffer want or be oppressed among them? And this seems to be pointed out by the circumstances which he describes; that it is the great duty, and ought to be the highest ambition of all governors, to order and establish such policy, and in such a wise manner, that every thing should be so managed, as to be conducive to the moral, temporal and eternal welfare of every individual from the lowest degree to the highest; and the consequence of this would be, the harmony, happiness and good prosperity of the whole community.

But this crafty author has also, in defence of his own or his employer's craft in the British West-India slavery, given sundry comparisons and descriptions of the treatment of slaves in the French islands and settlements in the West-Indies and America. And, contrary to what is the true case, he would have it supposed that the treatment of the slaves in the former, is milder than the latter; but even in this, unwarily for his own craft of slavery, all that he has advanced, can only add matter for its confutation, and serve to heighten the ardour and wish of every generous mind, that the whole should be abolished. An equal degree of enormity found in one place, cannot justify crimes of as great or greater enormity committed in another. The various depredations committed by robbers and plunderers, on different parts of the globe, may not be all equally alike bad, but their evil and malignancy, in every appearance and shape, can only hold up to view the just observation, that

Virtue herself hath such peculiar mein,
Vice, to be hated, needs but to be seen.

The farther and wider that the discovery and knowledge of such an enormous evil, as the base and villainous treatment and slavery which the poor unfortunate Black People meet with, is spread and made known, the cry for justice, even virtue lifting up her voice, must rise the louder and higher, for the scale of equity and justice to be lifted up in their defence. *And doth not wisdom cry, and understanding put forth her voice?* But who will regard the voice and hearken to the cry? Not the sneaking advocates for slavery, though a little ashamed of their craft; like the monstrous crocodile weeping over their prey with fine concessions (while gorging their own rapacious appetite) to hope for universal freedom taking place over the globe. Not those inebriated with avarice and infidelity, who hold in defiance every regard due to the divine law, and who endeavour all they can to destroy and take away the natural and common rights and privileges of men. Not the insolent and crafty author for slavery and oppression, who would have us to believe, that the benign command of God in appointing the seventh day for a sabbath of rest for the good purposes of our present and eternal welfare, is not to be regarded. He will exclaim against the teachers of obedience to it; and tells us, that the poor, and the oppressed, and the heavy burdened slave, should not lay down his load that day, but appropriate these hours of sacred rest to labour in some bit of useful ground. His own words are, "to dedicate the unappropriated hours of Sunday to the cultivation of this useful spot, he is brought up to believe would be the worst of sins, and that the sabbath is a day of absolute and universal rest is a truth he hears frequently inculcated by the curate of the parish," &c. But after bringing it about in this round-about way and manner, whatever the curate has to say of it as a truth, he would have us by no means to regard. This may serve as a specimen of his crafty and detestable production, where infidelity, false aspersions, virulent calumnies, and lying contradictions abound throughout. I shall only refer him to that description which he meant for another, as most applicable and best suited for himself; and so long as he does not renounce his craft, as well as to be somewhat ashamed of his craftsmen and their insensibility, he may thus stand as described by himself: "A man of warm imagination (but strange infatuated unfeeling sensibility) to paint things not as they really are, but as his rooted prejudices represent them, and even to shut his eyes against the convictions afforded him by his own senses."

But such is the insensibility of men, when their own craft of gain is advanced by the slavery and oppression of others, that after all the laudable exertions of the truly virtuous and humane, towards extending the beneficence of liberty and freedom to the much degraded and unfortunate Africans, which is the common right and privilege of all men, in every thing that is just, lawful and consistent, we find the principles of justice and equity, not only opposed, and every duty in religion and humanity left unregarded; but that unlawful traffic of dealing with our fellow-creatures, as with the beasts of the earth, still carried on with as great assiduity as ever; and that the insidious piracy of procuring and holding slaves is countenanced and supported by the government of sundry Christian nations. This seems to be the fashionable way of getting riches, but very dishonourable; in doing this, the slave-holders are meaner and baser than the African slaves, for while they subject and reduce them to a degree with brutes, they seduce themselves to a degree with devils.

"Some pretend that the Africans, in general, are a set of poor, ignorant, dispersed, unsociable people; and that they think it no crime to sell one another, and even their own wives and children; therefore they bring them away to a situation where many of them may arrive to a better state than ever they could obtain in their own native country." This specious pretence is without any shadow of justice and truth, and, if the argument was even true, it could afford no just and warrantable matter for any society of men to hold slaves. But the argument is false; there can be no ignorance, dispersion, or unsociableness so found among them, which can be made better by bringing them away to a state of a degree equal to that of a cow or a horse

But let their ignorance in some things (in which the Europeans have greatly the advantage of them) be what it will, it is not the intention of those who bring them away to make them better by it; nor is the design of slave-holders of any other intention, but that they may serve them as a kind of engines and beasts of burden; that their own ease and profit may be advanced, by a set of poor helpless men and women, whom they despise and rank with brutes, and keep them in perpetual slavery, both themselves and children, and merciful death is the only release from their toil. By the benevolence of some, a few may get their liberty, and by their own industry and ingenuity, may acquire some learning, mechanical trades, or useful business; and some may be brought away by different gentlemen to free countries, where they get their liberty; but no thanks to slave-holders for it. But amongst those who get their liberty, like all other ignorant men, are generally more corrupt in their morals, than they possibly could have been amongst their own people in Africa; for, being mostly amongst the wicked and apostate Christians, they sooner learn their oaths and blasphemies, and their evil ways, than any thing else. Some few, indeed, may eventually arrive at some knowledge of the Christian religion, and the great advantages of it. Such was the case of Ukawsaw Groniosaw, an African prince, who lived in England. He was a long time in a state of great poverty and distress, and must have died at one time for want, if a good and charitable Attorney had not supported him. He was long after in a very poor state, but he would not have given his faith in the Christian religion, in exchange for all the kingdoms of Africa, if they could have been given to him, in place of his poverty, for it. And such was A. Morrant in America. When a boy, he could stroll away into a desart, and prefer the society of wild beasts to the absurd Christianity of his mother's house. He was conducted to the king of the Cherokees, who, in a miraculous manner, was induced by him to embrace the Christian faith. This Morrant was in the British service last war, and his royal convert, the king of the Cherokee Indians, accompanied General Clinton at the siege of Charles-Town. These, and all such, I hope thousands, as meet with the knowledge and grace of the Divine clemency, are brought forth quite contrary to the end and intention of all slavery, and, in general, of all slave holders too. And should it please the Divine goodness to visit some of the poor dark Africans, even in the brutal stall of slavery, and from thence to instal them among the princes of his grace, and to invest them with a robe of honor that will hang about their necks for ever; but who can then suppose, that it will be well pleasing unto him to find them subjected there in that dejected state? Or can the slave-holders think that the Universal Father and Sovereign of Mankind will be well pleased with them, for the brutal transgression of his law, in bowing down the necks of those to the yoke of their cruel bondage? Sovereign goodness may eventually visit some men even in a state of slavery, but their slavery is not the cause of that event and benignity; and therefore, should some event of good ever happen to some men subjected to slavery, that can plead nothing for men to do evil that good may come; and should it apparently happen from thence, it is neither sought for nor designed by the enslavers of men. But the whole business of slavery is an evil of the first magnitude, and a most horrible iniquity to traffic with slaves and souls of men; and an evil sorry I am, that it still subsists, and more astonishing to think, that it is an iniquity committed amongst Christians, and contrary to all the genuine principles of Christianity, and yet carried on by men denominated thereby.

In a Christian æra, in a land where Christianity is planted, where every one might expect to behold the flourishing growth of every virtue, extending their harmonious branches with universal philanthropy wherever they came; but, on the contrary, almost nothing else is to be seen abroad but the bramble of ruffians, barbarians and slave-holders, grown up to a powerful luxuriance in wickedness. I cannot but wish, for the honor of Christianity, that the bramble grown up amongst them, was known to the heathen nations by a different name, for sure the depredators, robbers and ensnarers of men can never be Christians, but ought to be held as the abhorence of all men, and the abomination of all mankind, whether Christians or heathens. Every man of any sensibility, whether he be a Christian or an heathen, if he has any discernment at all, must think, that for any man, or any class of men, to deal with their fellow-creatures as with the beasts of the field; or to account them as such, however ignorant they may be, and in whatever situation, or wherever they may find them, and whatever country or complexion they may be of, that those men, who are the procurers and holders of slaves, are the greatest villains in the world. And surely those men must be lost to all sensibility themselves, who can think that the stealing, robbing, enslaving, and murdering of men can be no crimes; but the holders of men in slavery are at the head of all these oppressions and crimes. And, therefore, however unsensible they may be of it now, and however long they may laugh at the calamity of others, if they do not repent of their evil way, and the wickedness of their doings, by keeping and holding their fellow-creatures in slavery, and trafficking with them as with the brute creation, and to give up and surrender that evil traffic, with an awful abhorrence of it, that this may be averred, if they do not, and if they can think, they must and cannot otherwise but expect in one day at last, to meet with the full stroke of the long suspended vengeance of heaven, when death will cut them down to a state as mean as that of the most abjected slave, and to a very eminent danger of a far more dreadful fate hereafter, when they have the just reward of their iniquities to meet with.

And now, as to the Africans being dispersed and unsociable, if it was so, that could be no warrant for the Europeans to enslave them; and even though they may have many different feuds and bad practices among them, the continent of Africa is of vast extent, and the numerous inhabitants are divided into several kingdoms and principalities, which are governed by their respective kings and princes, and those are absolutely maintained by their free subjects. Very few nations make slaves of any of those under their government; but such as are taken prisoners of war from their neighbours, are generally kept in that state, until they can exchange and dispose of them otherwise; and towards the west coast they are generally procured for the European market, and sold. They have a great aversion to murder, or even in taking away the lives of those which they judge guilty of crimes; and, therefore, they prefer disposing of them otherwise better than killing them*. This gives their merchants and procurers of slaves a power to travel a great way into the interior parts of the country to buy such as are wanted to be disposed of. These slave-procurers are a set of as great villains as any in the world. They often steal and kidnap many more than they buy at first if they can meet with them by the way; and they have only their certain boundaries to go to, and sell them from one to another; so that if they are sought after and detected, the thieves are seldom found, and the others only plead that they bought them so and so. These kid-nappers and slave-procurers, called merchants, are a species of African villains, which are greatly corrupted, and even viciated by their intercourse with the Europeans; but, wicked and barbarous as they certainly are, I can hardly think, if they knew what horrible barbarity they were sending their fellow-creatures to, that they would do it. But the artful Europeans have so deceived them, that they are bought by their inventions of merchandize, and beguiled into it by their artifice; for the Europeans, at their factories, in some various manner, have always kept some as servants to them, and with gaudy cloaths, in a gay manner, as decoy ducks to deceive others, and to tell them that they want many more to go over the sea, and be as they are. So in that respect, wherein it may be said that they will sell one another, they are only ensnared and enlisted to be servants, kept like some of those which they see at the factories, which, for some gewgaws, as presents given to themselves and friends, they are thereby enticed to go; and something after the same manner that East-India soldiers are procured in Britain; and the inhabitants here, just as much sell themselves, and one another, as they do; and the kid-nappers here, and the slave-procurers in Africa, are much alike. But many other barbarous methods are made use of by the vile instigators, procurers and ensnarers of men; and some of the wicked and profligate princes and chiefs of Africa accept of presents, from the Europeans, to procure a certain number of slaves; and thereby they are wickedly instigated to go to war with one another on purpose to get them, which produces many terrible depredations; and sometimes when those engagements are entered into, and they find themselves de-

---

* It may be true, that some of the slaves transported from Africa, may have committed crimes in their own country, that require some slavery as a punishment; but, according to the laws of equity and justice, they ought to become free, as soon as their labour has paid their purchase in the West Indies or elsewhere.

feated of their purpose, it has happened that some of their own people have fallen a sacrifice to their avarice and cruelty. And it may be said of the Europeans, that they have made use of every insidious method to procure slaves whenever they can, and in whatever manner they can lay hold of them, and that their forts and factories are the avowed dens of thieves for robbers, plunderers and depredators.

But again, as to the Africans selling their own wives and children, nothing can be more opposite to every thing they hold dear and valuable; and nothing can distress them more, than to part with any of their relations and friends. Such are the tender feelings of parents for their children, that, for the loss of a child, they seldom can be rendered happy, even with the intercourse and enjoyment of their friends, for years. For any man to think that it should be otherwise, when he may see a thousand instances of a natural instinct, even in the brute creation, where they have a sympathetic feeling for their offspring; it must be great want of consideration not to think, that much more than meerly what is natural to animals, should in a higher degree be implanted in the breast of every part of the rational creation of man. And what man of feeling can help lamenting the loss of parents, friends, liberty, and perhaps property and other valuable and dear connections. Those people annually brought away from Guinea, are born as free, and are brought up with as great a predilection for their own country, freedom and liberty, as the sons and daughters of fair Britain. Their free subjects are trained up to a kind of military service, not so much by the desire of the chief, as by their own voluntary inclination. It is looked upon as the greatest respect they can shew to their king, to stand up for his and their own defence in time of need. Their different chieftains, which bear a reliance on the great chief, or king, exercise a kind of government something like that feudal institution which prevailed some time in Scotland. In this respect, though the common people are free, they often suffer by the villainy of their different chieftains, and by the wars and feuds which happen among them. Nevertheless their freedom and rights are as dear to them, as those privileges are to other people. And it may be said that freedom, and the liberty of enjoying their own privileges, burns with as much zeal and fervour in the breast of an Aethiopian, as in the breast of any inhabitant on the globe.

But the supporters and favourers of slavery make other things a pretence and an excuse in their own defence; such as, that they find that it was admitted under the Divine institution by Moses, as well as the long continued practice of different nations for ages; and that the Africans are peculiarly marked out by some signal prediction in nature and complexion for that purpose.

This seems to be the greatest bulwark of defence which the advocates and favourers of slavery can advance, and what is generally talked of in their favour by those who do not understand it. I shall consider it in that view, whereby it will appear, that they deceive themselves and mislead others. Men are never more liable to be drawn into error, than when truth is made use of in a guileful manner to seduce them. Those who do not believe the scriptures to be a Divine revelation, cannot, consistently with themselves, make the law of Moses, or any mark or prediction they can find respecting any particular set of men, as found in the sacred writings, any reason that one class of men should enslave another. In that respect, all that they have to enquire into should be, whether it be right, or wrong, that any part of the human species should enslave another; and when that is the case, the Africans, though not so learned, are just as wise as the Europeans; and when the matter is left to human wisdom, they are both liable to err. But what the light of nature, and the dictates of reason, when rightly considered, teach, is, that no man ought to enslave another; and some, who have been rightly guided thereby, have made noble defences for the universal natural rights and privileges of all men. But in this case, when the learned take neither revelation nor reason for their guide, they fall into as great, and worse errors, than the unlearned; for they only make use of that system of Divine wisdom, which should guide them into truth, when they can find or pick out any thing that will suit their purpose, or that they can pervert to such—the very means of leading themselves and others into error. And, in consequence thereof, the pretences that some men make use of for holding of slaves, must be evidently the grossest perversion of reason, as well as an inconsistent and diabolical use of the sacred writings. For it must be a strange perversion of reason, and a wrong use or disbelief of the sacred writings, when any thing found there is so perverted by them, and set up as a precedent and rule for men to commit wickedness. They had better have no reason, and no belief in the scriptures, and make no use of them at all, than only to believe, and make use of that which leads them into the most abominable evil and wickedness of dealing unjustly with their fellow men.

But this will appear evident to all men that believe the scriptures, that every reason necessary is given that they should be believed; and, in this case, that they afford us this information: "That all mankind did spring from one original, and that there are no different species among men. For God who made the world, hath made of one blood all the nations of men that dwell on all the face of the earth." Wherefore we may justly infer, as there are no inferior species, but all of one blood and of one nature, that there does not an inferiority subsist, or depend, on their colour, features or form, whereby some men make a pretence to enslave others; and consequently, as they have all one creator, one original, made of one blood, and all brethren descended from one father, it never could be lawful and just for any nation, or people, to oppress and enslave another.

And again, as all the present inhabitants of the world sprang from the family of Noah, and were then all of one complexion, there is no doubt, but the difference which we now find, took its rise very rapidly after they became dispersed and settled on the different parts of the globe. There seems to be a tendency to this, in many instances, among children of the same parents, having different colour of hair and features from one another. And God alone who established the course of nature, can bring about and establish what variety he pleases; and it is not in the power of man to make one hair white or black. But among the variety which it hath pleased God to establish and caused to take place, we may meet with some analogy in nature, that as the bodies of men are tempered with a different degree to enable them to endure the respective climates of their habitations, so their colours vary, in some degree, in a regular gradation from the equator towards either of the poles. However, there are other incidental causes arising from time and place, which constitute the most distinguishing variety of colour, form appearance and features, as peculiar to the inhabitants of one tract of country, and differing in something from those in another, even in the same latitudes, as well as from those in different climates. Long custom and the different way of living among the several inhabitants of the different parts of the earth, has a very great effect in distinguishing them by a difference of features and complexion. These effects are easy to be seen; as to the causes, it is sufficient for us to know, that all is the work of an Almighty hand. Therefore, as we find the distribution of the human species inhabiting the barren, as well as the most fruitful parts of the earth, and the cold as well as the most hot, differing from one another in complexion according to their situation; it may be reasonably, as well as religiously, inferred, that He who placed them in their various situations, hath extended equally his care and protection to all; and from thence, that it becometh unlawful to counteract his benignity, by reducing others of different complexions to undeserved bondage.

According, as we find that the difference of colour among men is only incidental, and equally natural to all, and agreeable to the place of their habitation; and that if nothing else be different or contrary among them, but that of features and complexion, in that respect, they are all equally alike entitled to the enjoyment of every mercy and blessing of God. But there are some men of that complexion, because they are not black, whose ignorance and insolence leads them to think, that those who are black, were marked out in that manner by some signal interdiction or curse, as originally descending from their progenitors. To those I must say, that the only mark which we read of, as generally alluded to, and by them applied wrongfully, is that mark or sign which God gave to Cain, to assure him that he should not be destroyed. Cain understood by the nature of the crime he had committed, that the law required death, or cutting off, as the punishment thereof. But God in his providence doth not always punish the wicked in this life according to their enormous crimes, (we are told, by a sacred poet, that he saw the wicked flourishing like a green bay tree) though he generally marks them out by some signal token of his vengeance; and that is a sure token of it, when men become long hardened in their wickedness. The denunciation that passed upon Cain was, that he should be a fugitive and a vagabond on the earth, bearing the curse and reproach of his iniquity; and the rest of men were prohibited as much from meddling with him, or defiling their hands by him, as it naturally is, not to pull down the dead carcase of an atrocious criminal, hung up in chains by the laws of his country. But allow the mark set upon Cain to have consisted in a black skin, still no conclusion can be drawn at all, that any of the black people are of that descent, as the whole posterity of Cain were destroyed in the universal deluge.

Only Noah, a righteous and just man, who found grace in the sight of God, and his three sons, Japheth, Shem and Ham, and their wives, eight persons, were preserved from the universal deluge, in the ark which Noah was directed to build. The three sons of Noah had each children born after the flood, from whom all the present world of men descended. But it came to pass, in the days of Noah, that an interdiction, or curse, took place in the family of Ham, and that the descendants of one of his sons should become the servants of servants to their brethren, the descendants of Shem and Japheth. This affords a grand pretence for the supporters of the African slavery to build a false notion upon, as it is found by history that Africa, in general, was peopled by the descendants of Ham; but they forget, that the prediction has already been fulfilled as far as it can go.

There can be no doubt, that there was a shameful misconduct in Ham himself, by what is related of him; but the fault, according to the prediction and curse, descended only to the families of the descendants of his youngest son, Canaan. The occasion was, that Noah, his father, had drank wine, and (perhaps unawares) became inebriated by it, and fell asleep in his tent. It seems that Ham was greatly deficient of that filial virtue as either becoming a father or a son, went into his father's tent, and, it may be supposed, in an undecent manner, he had suffered his own son, Canaan, so to meddle with, or uncover, his father, that he saw his nakedness; for which he did not check the audacious rudeness of Canaan, but went and told his brethren without in ridicule of his aged parent. This rude audacious behaviour of Canaan, and the obloquy of his father Ham, brought on him the curse of his grandfather, Noah, but he blessed Shem and Japheth for their decent and filial virtues, and denounced, in the spirit of prophecy, that Canaan should be their servant, and should serve them.

It may be observed; that it is a great misfortune for children, when their parents are not endowed with that wisdom and prudence which is necessary for the early initiation of their offspring in the paths of virtue and righteousness. Ham was guilty of the offence as well as his son; he did not pity the weakness of his father, who was overcome with wine in that day wherein, it is likely, he had some solemn work to do. But the prediction and curse rested wholly upon the offspring of Canaan, who settled in the land known by his name, in the west of Asia, as is evident from the sacred writings. The Canaanites became an exceeding wicked people, and were visited with many calamities, according to the prediction of Noah, for their abominable wickedness and idolatry.

Chederluomer, a descendant of Shem, reduced the Canaanitish kingdoms to a tributary subjection; and some time after, upon their revolt, invaded and pillaged their country. Not long after Sodom, Gomorrah, Admah and Zeboim, four kingdoms of the Canaanites were overthrown for their great wickedness, and utterly destroyed by fire and brimstone from heaven. The Hebrews, chiefly under Moses, Joshua and Barak, as they were directed by God, cut off most of the other

Canaanitish kingdoms, and reduced many of them to subjection and vassalage. Those who settled in the north-west of Canaan, and formed the once flourishing states of Tyre and Sidon, were by the Assyrians, the Chaldeans, and the Persians successively reduced to great misery and bondage; but chiefly by the Greeks, the Romans, and the Saracens, and lastly by the Turks, they were compleatly and totally ruined, and have no more since been a distinct people among the different nations. Many of the Canaanites who fled away in the Time of Joshua, became mingled with the different nations, and some historians think that some of them came to England, and settled about Cornwall, as far back as that time; so that, for any thing that can be known to the contrary, there may be some of the descendants of that wicked generation still subsisting among the slave-holders in the West-Indies. For if the curse of God ever rested upon them, or upon any other men, the only visible mark thereof was always upon those who committed the most outrageous acts of violence and oppression. But colour and complexion has nothing to do with that mark; every wicked man, and the enslavers of others, bear the stamp of their own iniquity, and that mark which was set upon Cain.

Now, the descendants of the other three sons of Ham, were not included under the curse of his father, and as they dispersed and settled on the different parts of the earth, they became also sundry distinct and very formidable nations. Cush, the oldest, settled in the south-west of Arabia, and his descendants were anciently known to the Hebrews by the name of Cushites, or Cushie; one of his sons, Nimrod, founded the kingdom of Babylon, in Asia; and the others made their descent southward, by the Red Sea, and came over to Abyssinia and Ethiopia, and, likely, dispersed themselves throughout all the southern and interior parts of Africa; and as they lived mostly under the torrid zone, or near the tropics, they became black, as being natural to the inhabitants of those sultry hot climates; and, in that case, their complexion bears the signification of the name of their original progenitor, Cush, as known by the Hebrews by that name, both on the east and on the west, beyond the Red Sea; but the Greeks called them Ethiopians, or black faced people. The Egyptians and Philistines were the descendants of Mizraim, and the country which they inhabited was called the land of Mizraim, and Africa, in general, was anciently called the whole land of Ham. Phut, another of his sons, also settled on the west of Egypt, and as the youngest were obliged to emigrate farthest, afterwards dispersed themselves chiefly up the south of the Mediterranean sea, towards Lybia and Mauritania, and might early mingle with some of the Cushites on the more southern, and, chiefly, on the western parts of Africa. But all these might be followed by some other families and tribes from Asia; and some think that Africa got its name from the King of Lybia marrying a daughter of Aphra, one of the descendants of Abraham, by Keturah.

But it may be reasonably supposed, that the most part of the black people in Africa, are the descendants of the Cushites, towards the east, the south, and interior parts, and chiefly of the Phutians towards the west; and the various revolutions and changes which have happened among them have rather been local than universal; so that whoever their original progenitors were, as descending from one generation to another, in a long continuance, it becomes natural for the inhabitants of that tract of country to be a dark black, in general. The learned and thinking part of men, who can refer to history, must know, that nothing with respect to colour, nor any mark or curse from any original prediction, can in anywise be more particularly ascribed to the Africans than to any other people of the human species, so as to afford any pretence why they should be more evil treated, persecuted and enslaved, than any other. Nothing but ignorance, and the dreams of a viciated imagination, arising from the general countenance given to the evil practice of wicked men, to strengthen their hands in wickedness, could ever make any person to fancy otherwise, or ever to think that the stealing, kidnapping, enslaving, persecuting or killing a black man, is in any way and manner less criminal, than the same evil treatment of any other man of another complexion.

But again, in answer to another part of the pretence which the favourers of slavery make use of in their defence, that slavery was an ancient custom, and that it became the prevalent and universal practice of many different barbarous nations for ages: This must be granted; but not because it was right, or any thing like right and equity. A lawful servitude was always necessary, and became contingent with the very nature of human society. But when the laws of civilization were broken through, and when the rights and properties of others were invaded, that brought the oppressed into a kind of compulsive servitude, though often not compelled to it by those whom they were obliged to serve. This arose from the different depredations and robberies which were committed upon one another; the helpless were obliged to seek protection from such as could support them, and to give unto them their service, in order to preserve themselves from want, and to deliver them from the injury either of men or beasts. For while civil society continued in a rude state, even among the establishers of kingdoms, when they became powerful and proud, as they wanted to enlarge their territories, they drove and expelled others from their peaceable habitations, who were not so powerful as themselves. This made those who were robbed of their substance, and drove from the place of their abode, make their escape to such as could and would help them; but when such a relief could not be found, they were obliged to submit to the yoke of their oppressors, who, in many cases, would not yield them any protection upon any terms. Wherefore, when their lives were in danger otherwise, and they could not find any help, they were obliged to sell themselves for bond servants to such as would buy them, when they could not get a service that was better. But as soon as buyers could be found, robbers began their traffic to ensnare others, and such as fell into their hands were carried captive by them, and were obliged to submit to their being sold by them into the hands of other robbers, for there are few buyers of men, who intend thereby to make them free, and such as they buy are generally subjected to hard labour and bondage. Therefore at all times, while a man is a slave, he is still in captivity, and under the jurisdiction of robbers; and every man who keeps a slave, is a robber, whenever he compels him to his service without giving him a just reward. The barely supplying his slave with some necessary things, to keep him in life, is no reward at all, that is only for his own sake and benefit; and the very nature of compulsion and taking away the liberty of others, as well as their property, is robbery; and that kind of service which subjects men to a state of slavery, must at all times, and in every circumstance, be a barbarous, inhuman and unjust dealing with our fellow men. A voluntary service, and slavery, are quite different things; but in ancient times, in whatever degree slavery was admitted, and whatever hardships they were, in general, subjected to, it was not nearly so bad as the modern barbarous and cruel West-India slavery.

Now, in respect to that kind of servitude which was admitted into the law of Moses, that was not contrary to the natural liberties of men, but a state of equity and justice, according as the nature and circumstances of the times required. There was no more harm in entering into a covenant with another man as a bond-servant, than there is for two men to enter into partnership the one with the other; and sometimes the nature of the case may be, and their business require it, that the one may find money and live at a distance and ease, and the other manage the business for him: So a bond-servant was generally the steward in a man's house, and sometimes his heir. There was no harm in buying a man who was in a state of captivity and bondage by others, and keeping him in servitude till such time as his purchase was redeemed by his labour and service. And there could be no harm in paying a man's debts, and keeping him in servitude until such time as an equitable agreement of composition was paid by him. And so, in general, whether they had been bought or sold in order to pay their just debts when they became poor, or were bought from such as held them in an unlawful captivity, the state of bondage which they and their children fell under, among the Israelites, was into that of a vassalage state, which rather might be termed a deliverance from debt and captivity, than a state of slavery. In that vassalage state which they were reduced to, they had a tax of some service to pay, which might only be reckoned equivalent to a poor man in England paying rent for his cottage. In this fair land of liberty, there are many thousands of the inhabitants who have no right to so much land as an inch of ground to set their foot upon, so as to take up their residence upon it, without paying a lawful and reasonable vassalage of rent for it—and yet the whole community is free from slavery. And so, likewise, those who were reduced to a state of servitude, or vassalage, in the land of Israel, were not negociable like chattels and goods; nor could they be disposed of like cattle and beasts of burden, or ever transferred or disposed of without their own consent; and perhaps not one man in all the land of Israel would buy another man, unless that man was willing to serve him. And when any man had gotten such a servant, as he had entered into a covenant of agreement with, as a bond-servant, if the man liked his master and his service, he could not oblige him to go away; and it sometimes happened, that they refused to go out free when the year of jubilee came. But even that state of servitude which the Canaanites were reduced to, among those who survived the general overthrow of their country, was nothing worse, in many respects, than that of poor labouring people in any free country. Their being made hewers of wood and drawers of water, were laborious employments; but they were paid for it in such a manner as the nature of their service required, and were supplied with abundance of such necessaries of life as they and their families had need of; and they were at liberty, if they chose, to go away, there was no restriction laid on them. They were not hunted after, and a reward offered for their heads, as it is the case in the West-Indies for any that can find a strayed slave; and he who can bring such a head warm reeking with his blood, as a token that he had murdered him—inhuman and shocking to think!—he is paid for it; and, cruel and dreadful as it is, that law is still in force in some of the British colonies.

But the Canaanites, although they were predicted to be reduced to a state of servitude, and bondage to that poor and menial employment, fared better than the West-India slaves; for when they were brought into that state of servitude, they were often employed in an honourable service. The Nethenims, and others, were to assist in the sacred solemnities and worship of God at the Temple of Jerusalem. They had the same laws and immunities respecting the solemn days and sabbaths, as their masters the Israelites, and they were to keep and observe them. But they were not suffered, much less required, to labour in their own spots of useful ground on the days of sacred rest from worldly employment; and that, if they did not improve the culture of it, in these times and seasons, they might otherwise perish for hunger and want; as it is the case of the West-India slaves, by their inhuman, infidel, hard-hearted masters. And, therefore, this may be justly said, that whatever servitude that was, or by whatever name it may be called, that the service which was required by the people of Israel in old time, was of a far milder nature, than that which became the prevalent practice of other different and barbarous nations; and, if compared with modern slavery, it might be called liberty, equity, and felicity, in respect to that abominable, mean, beastly, cruel, bloody slavery carried on by the inhuman, barbarous Europeans, against the poor unfortunate Black Africans.

But again, this may be averred, that the servitude which took place under the sanction of the divine law, in the time of Moses, and what was enjoined as the civil and religious polity of the people of Israel, was in nothing contrary to the natural rights and common liberties of men, though it had an appearance as such for great and wise ends. The Divine Law Giver, in his good providence, for great and wise purposes intended by it, has always admitted into the world riches and poverty, prosperity and adversity, high and low, rich and poor; and in such manner, as in all their variety and difference, mutation and change, there is nothing set forth in the written law, by Moses, contrary, unbecoming, or inconsistent with that goodness of himself, as the wise and righteous Governor of the Universe. Those things admitted into the law, that had a seeming appearance contrary to the natural liberties of men, were only so admitted for a local time, to point out, and to establish, and to give instruction thereby, in an analogous allusion to other things.

And therefore, so far as I have been able to consult the law written by Moses, concerning that kind of servitude admitted by it, I can find nothing imported thereby, in the least degree, to warrant the modern practice of slavery. But, on the contrary, and what was principally intended thereby, and in the most particular manner, as respecting Christians, that it contains the strongest prohibition against it. And every Christian man, that can read his Bible, may find that which is of the greatest importance for himself to know, implied even under the very institution of bond-servants; and that the state of bondage which the law denounces and describes, was thereby so intended to point out something necessary, as well as similar to all the other ritual and ceremonial services; and that the whole is set forth in such a manner, as containing the very essence and foundation of the Christian religion. And, moreover, that it must appear evident to any Christian believer, that it was necessary that all these things should take place, and as the most beautiful fabric of Divine goodness, that in all their variety, and in all their forms, they should stand recorded under the sanction of the Divine law.

And this must be observed, that it hath so pleased the Almighty Creator, to establish all the variety of things in nature, different complexions and other circumstances among men, and to record the various transactions of his own providence, with all the ceremonial œconomy written in the books of Moses, as more particularly respecting and enjoined to the Israelitish nation and people, for the use of sacred language, in order to convey wisdom to the fallen apostate human race. Wherefore, all the various things established, admitted and recorded, whether natural, moral, typical or ceremonial, with all the various things in nature referred to, were so ordered and admitted, as figures, types and emblems, and other symbolical representations, to bring forward, usher in, hold forth and illustrate that most amazing transaction, and the things concerning it, of all things the most wonderful that ever could take place amongst the universe of intelligent beings; as in that, and the things concerning it, of the salvation of apostate men, and the wonderful benignity of their Almighty Redeemer.

Whoever will give a serious and unprejudiced attention to the various things alluded to in the language of sacred writ, must see reason to believe that they imply a purpose and design far more glorious and important, than what seems generally to be understood by them; and to point to objects and events far more extensive and interesting, than what is generally ascribed to them. But as the grand eligibility and importance of those things, implied and pointed out in sacred writ, and the right understanding thereof, belongs to the sublime science of metaphysics and theology to enforce, illustrate and explain, I shall only select a few instances, which I think have a relation to my subject in hand.

Among other things it may be considered, that the different colours and complexions among men were intended for another purpose and design, than that of being only eligible in the variety of the scale of nature. And, accordingly, had it been otherwise, and if there had never been any black people among the children of men, nor any spotted leopards among the beasts of the earth, such an instructive question, by the prophet, could not have been proposed, as this, *Can the Ethiopian change his skin, or the leopard his spots? Then, may ye also do good, that are accustomed to do evil.* Jer. xiii.23. The instruction intended by this is evident, that it was a convincing and forcible argument to shew, that none among the fallen and apostate race of men, can by any effort of their own, change their nature from the blackness and guilt of the sable dye of sin and polution, or alter their way accustomed to do evil, from the variegated spots of their iniquity; and that such a change is as impossible to be totally and radically effected by them, as it is for a black man to change the colour of his skin, or the leopard to alter his spots. But these differences of a natural variety amongst the things themselves, is in every respect equally innocent, and what they cannot alter or change, was made to be so, and in the most eligible and primary design, were so intended for the very purposes of instructive language to men. And by these extreme differences of colour, it was intended to point out and shew to the white man, that there is a sinful blackness in his own nature, which he can no more change, than the external blackness which he sees in another can be rendered otherwise; and it likewise holds out to the black man, that the sinful blackness of his own nature is such, that he can no more alter, than the outward appearance of his colour can be brought to that of another. And this is imported by it, that there is an inherent evil in every man, contrary to that which is good; and that all men are like Ethiopians (even God's elect) in a state of nature and unregeneracy, they are black with original sin, and spotted with actual transgression, which they cannot reverse. But to this truth, asserted of blackness, I must add another glorious one. All thanks and eternal praise be to God! His infinite wisdom and goodness has found out a way of renovation, and has opened a fountain through the blood of Jesus, for sin and for uncleanness, wherein all the stains and blackest dyes of sin and polution can be washed away for ever, and the darkest sinner be made to shine as the brightest angel in heaven. And for that end and purpose, God alone has appointed all the channels of conveyance of the everlasting Gospel for these healing and purifying streams of the water of life to run in, and to bring life and salvation, with light and gladness to men; but he denounces woe to those who do not receive it themselves, but hinder and debar others who would, from coming to those salutary streams for life: Yet not alone confined to these, nor hindered in his purpose by any opposers, HE, who can open the eyes of the blind, and make the deaf to hear, can open streams in the desart, and make his benignity to flow, and his salvation to visit, even the meanest and most ignorant man, in the darkest shades of nature, as well as the most learned on the earth; and he usually carries on his own gracious work of quickening and redeeming grace, in a secret, sovereign manner. To this I must again observe, and what I chiefly intended by this similitude, that the external blackness of the Ethiopians, is as innocent and natural, as spots in the leopards; and that the difference of colour and complexion, which in hath pleased God to appoint among men, are no more unbecoming unto either of them, than the different shades of the rainbow are unseemly to the whole, or unbecoming to any part of that apparent arch. It does not alter the nature and quality of a man, whether he wears a black or a white coat, whether he puts it on or strips it off, he is still the same man. And so likewise, when a man comes to die, it makes no difference whether he was black or white, whether he was male or female, whether he was great or small, or whether he was old or young; none of these differences alter the essentiality of the man, any more than he had wore a black or a white coat and thrown it off for ever.

Another form of instruction for the same purpose, may be taken from the slavery and oppression which men have committed upon one another, as well as that kind of bondage and servitude which was admitted under the sanction of the Divine law. But there is nothing set

forth in the law as a rule, or any thing recorded therein that can stand
as a precedent, or make it lawful, for men to practice slavery; nor can
any laws in favour of slavery be deduced from thence, for to enslave
men, be otherwise, than as unwarrantble, as it would be unnecessary
and wrong, to order and command the sacrifices of beasts to be still
continued. Now the great thing imported by it, and what is chiefly to
be deduced from it in this respect, is, that so far as the law concerning
bond-servants, and that establishment of servitude, as admitted in the
Mosaical institution, was set forth, it was thereby intended to prefigure
and point out, that spiritual subjection and bondage to sin, that all
mankind, by their original transgression, were fallen into. All men in
their fallen depraved state, being under a spirit of bondage, sunk into
a nature of brutish carnality, and by the lusts thereof, they are carried
captive and enslaved; and the consequence is, that they are sold under
sin and in bondage to iniquity, and carried captive by the devil at his
will. This being the case, the thing proves itself; for if there had been
no evil and sin amongst men, there never would have been any kind of
bondage, slavery and oppression found amongst them; and if there was
none of these things to be found, the great cause of it could not, in the
present situation of men, be pointed out to them in that eligible manner as it is. Wherefore it was necessary that something of that bondage
and servitude should be admitted into the ritual law for a figurative
use, which, in all other respects and circumstances, was, in itself, contrary to the whole tenure of the law, and naturally in itself unlawful for
men to practice.

Nothing but heavenly wisdom, and heavenly grace, can teach men
to understand. The most deplorable of all things is, that the dreadful
situation of our universalde praved state, which all mankind lyeth under, is such, that those who are not redeemed in time, must for ever
continue to be the subjects of eternal bondage and misery. Blessed be
God! he hath appointed and set up a deliverance, and the Saviour of
Men is an Almighty Redeemer. When God, the Almighty Redeemer
and Saviour of his people, brought his Israel out of Egypt and temporal
bondage, it was intended and designed thereby, to set up an emblematical representation of their deliverance from the power and captivity of
sin, and from the dominion of that evil and malignant spirit, who had
with exquisite subtilty and guile at first seduced the original progenitors of mankind. And when they were brought to the promised land,
and had gotten deliverance, and subdued their enemies under them,

they were to reign over them; and their laws respecting bond-servants, and other things of that nature, were to denote, that they were to keep under and in subjection the whole body of their evil affections and lusts. This is so declared by the Apostle, that the law is spiritual, and intended for spiritual uses. The general state of slavery which took place in the world, among other enormous crimes of wicked men might have served for an emblem and similitude of our spiritual bondage and slavery to sin; but, unless it had been admitted into the spiritual and divine law, it could not have stood and become an emblem that there was any spiritual restoration and deliverance afforded to us. By that which is evil in captivity and slavery among men, we are thereby so represented to be under a like subjection to sin; but by what is instituted in the law by Moses, in that respect we are thereby represented as Israel to have dominion over sin, and to rule over and keep in subjection all our spiritual enemies. And, therefore, any thing which had a seeming appearance in favour of slavery, so far as it was admitted into the law, was to shew that it was not natural and innocent, like that of different colours among men, but as necessary to be made an emblem of what was intended by it, and, consequently, as it stands enjoined among other typical representations, was to shew that every thing of any evil appearance of it, was to be removed, and to end with the other typical and ceremonial injunctions, when the time of that dispensation was over. This must appear evident to all Christian believers; and since therefore all these things are fulfilled in the establishment of Christianity, there is now nothing remaining in the law for a rule of practice to men, but the ever abiding obligations, and ever binding injunctions of moral rectitude, justice, equity and righteousness. All the other things in the Divine law, are for spiritual uses and similitudes, for giving instruction to the wise, and understanding to the upright in heart, that the man of God may be perfect, throughly furnished unto all good works.

Among other things also, the wars of the Israelites, and the extirpation of the Canaanites, and other circumstances as recorded in sacred history, were intended to give instruction to men, but have often been perverted to the most flagrant abuse, and even inverted to the most notorious purposes, for men to embolden themselves to commit wickedness. Every possession that men enjoy upon earth are the gifts of God, and he who gives them, may either take them away again from men, or he may take men away themselves from the earth, as it pleaseth him. But who dare, even with Lucifer, the malignant devourer of the world, think to imitate the most High? The extirpation of the Canaanites out of their land, was so ordered, not only to punish them for their idolatry and abominable wickedness, but also to shew forth the honour of his power, and the sovereignty of him who is the only potent one that reigneth over the nations; that all men at that time might learn to fear and know him who is Jehovah; and ever since that it might continue a standing memorial of him, and a standard of honor unto him who doth according to his will among the armies of heaven, and whatever pleaseth him with the inhabitants of the earth. And, in general, these transactions stand recorded for an emblematical use and similitude, in the spiritual warfare of every true Israelite throughout all the ages of time. Every real believer and valiant champion in the knowledge and faith of their Omnipotent Saviour and Almighty Deliverer, as the very nature of Christianity requires and enjoins, knoweth the use of these things, *and they know how to endure hardness as good soldiers of Jesus Christ.* They have many battles to fight with their unbelief, the perverseness of their nature, evil tempers and besetting sins, these Canaanites which still dwell in their land. They are so surrounded with adversaries, that they have need always to be upon their guard, and to have all their armour on. They are *commanded to cast off the works of darkness, and to put on the whole armour of righteousness and light; and that they may be strong in the Lord, and in the power of his might.* For it is required *that they should be able to stand against the wiles of the devil, the powers of the rulers of the darkness of this world, against spiritual wickedness in high places.* And as their foes are *mighty and tall like the Anakims, and fenced up to heaven, they must be mighty warriors, men of renown, valiant for the truth, strong in the faith, fighting the Lord's battles, and overcoming all their enemies, through the dear might of the Great Captain of their salvation.* In this warfare, should they meet with some mighty Agag, some strong corruption, or besetting sin, they are commanded to cut it down, and with the sword of Samuel to hew it to pieces before the Lord. This, in its literal sense, may seem harsh, as if Samuel had been cruel; and so will our sins, and other sinners insinuate and tell us not to mind such things as the perfect law of God requires. But if we consider that the Lord God who breathed into man the breath of life, can suspend and take it away when he pleaseth, and that there is not a moment we have to exist, wherein that life may not be suspended before the next: it was therefore of an indifferent matter for that man Agag, when the Lord, who hath the breath and life of every man in his hand, had appointed him at that time to die, for his great wickedness and the murders committed by him, whether he was slain by Samuel or any other means. But what Samuel, the servant of the Lord, did in that instance, was in obedience to his voice, and in itself a righteous deed, and a just judgment upon Agag. And the matter imported by it, was also intended to shew, that all our Amalekite sins, and even the chief and darling of them, the avaricious and covetous Agags, should be cut off for ever. But if we spare them, and leave them to remain alive in stubborn disobedience to the law and commandments of God, we should in that case, be like Saul, cut off ourselves from the kingdom of his grace. According to this view, it may suffice to shew (and what infinite wisdom intended, no doubt,) that a wise and righteous use may be made of those very things, which otherwise are generally perverted to wrong purposes.

And now, as to these few instances which I have collected from that sacred hypothesis, whereby it is shewn, that other things are implied and to be understood by the various incidents as recorded in sacred writ, with a variety of other things in nature, bearing an analogous allusion to things of the greatest importance for every Christian man to know and understand; and that the whole of the ritual law, though these things themselves are not to be again repeated, is of that nature and use as never to be forgot. And therefore to suppose, or for any Christians to say, that they have nothing to do with those things now in the right use thereof, and what was intended and imported thereby respecting themselves, would be equally as absurd as to hear them speaking in the language of devils; and they might as well say as they did, when speaking out of the demoniac, that they have nothing to do with Christ.

Having thus endeavoured to shew, and what, I think, must appear evident and obvious, that none of all these grand pretensions, as generally made use of by the favourers of slavery, to encourage and embolden them, in that iniquitous traffic, can have any foundation or shadow of truth to support them; and that there is nothing in nature, reason, and scripture can be found, in any manner or way, to warrant the enslaving of black people more than others.

But I am aware that some of these arguments will weigh nothing against such men as do not believe the scriptures themselves, nor care to understand; but let them be aware not to make use of these things against us which they do not believe, or whatever pretence they may have for committing violence against us. Any property taken away from others, whether by stealth, fraud, or violence, must be wrong; but to take away men themselves, and keep them in slavery, must be worse. *Skin for skin, all that a man hath would be give for his life*; and would rather lose his property to any amount whatever, than to have his liberty taken away, and be kept as a slave. It must be an inconceivable fallacy to think otherwise: none but the inconsiderate, most obdurate and stubborn, could ever think that it was right to enslave others. *But the way of the wicked is brutish: his own iniquity shall take the wicked himself, and he shall be holden with the cords of his sins: he shall die without instruction, and in the greatness of his folly he shall go astray.*

Among the various species of men that commit rapine, and violence, and murders, and theft, upon their fellow-creatures, like the ravenous beasts of the night, prowling for their prey, there are also those that set out their heads in the open day, opposing all the obligations of civilization among men, and breaking through all the laws of justice and equity to them, and making even the very things which are analogous to the obligations, which ought to warn and prohibit them, a pretence for their iniquity and injustice. Such are the insidious merchants and pirates that gladen their oars with the carnage and captivity of men, and the vile negociators and enslavers of the human species. The prohibitions against them are so strong, that, in order to break through and to commit the most notorious and flagrant crimes with impunity, they are obliged to oil their poisonous pretences with various perversions of sundry transactions of things even in sacred writ, that the acrimonious points of their arsenic may be swallowed down the better, and the evil effects of their crimes appear the less. In this respect, instead of *the sacred history of the Israelitish nation being made profitable to them, for doctrine, for reproof, for correction, and for instruction in righteousness*, as it was intended, *and given to men* for that purpose; but, instead thereof, the wars of the Israelites, the extirpation and subjection of the Canaanites, and other transactions of that kind, are generally made use of by wicked men as precedents and pretences to encourage and embolden themselves to commit cruelty and slavery on their fellow-creatures: and the merciless depredators, negociators, and enslavers of men, revert to the very ritual law of Moses as a precedent for their barbarity, cruelty, and injustice; which law, though devoid of any iniquity, as bearing a parallel allusion to other things signified thereby, can afford no precedent for their evil way, in any shape or view: what was intended by it is fulfilled, and in no respect, or any thing like it, can be repeated again, without transgressing and breaking through every other injunction, precept, and command of the just and tremendous law of God.

The consequence of their apostacy from God, and disobedience to his law, became a snare to those men in times of old, who departed from it; and because of their disobedience and wickedness, the several nations, which went astray after their own abominations, were visited with many dreadful calamities and judgments. But to set up the ways of the wicked for an example, and to make the laws respecting their suppression, and the judgments that were inflicted upon them for their iniquity, and even the written word of God, and the transactions of his providence, to be reversed and become and precedents and pretences for men to commit depredations and extirpations, and for enslaving and negociating or merchandizing the human species, must be horrible wickedness indeed, and sinning with a high hand. And it cannot be thought otherwise, but that the abandoned aggressors, among the learned nations will, in due time, as the just reward of their aggravated iniquity, be visited with some more dreadful and tremendous judgments of the righteous vengeance of God, than what even befel to the Canaanites of old.

And it may be considered further, that to draw any inferences in favour of extirpation, slavery, and negociation of men, from the written word of God, or from any thing else in the history and customs of different nations, as a precedent to embolden wicked men in their wickedness; cannot be more wicked, ridiculous, and absurd to shew any favour to these insidious negociators and enslavers, than it would be to stand and laugh, and look on with a brutal and savage impunity, at beholding the following supposition transacted. Suppose two or three half-witted foolish fellows happened to come past a crowd of people, gazing at one which they had hung up by the neck on a tree, as a victim suffering for breaking the laws of his country; and suppose these foolish fellows went on a little way in a bye path, and found some innocent person, not suspecting any harm till taken hold of by them, and could not deliver himself from them, and just because they had seen among the crowd of people which they came past, that there had been a man hung by the neck, they took it into their foolish wicked heads to hang up the poor innocent man on the next tree, and just did as they had seen others do, to please their own fancy and base foolishness, to see how he would swing. Now if any of the other people happened to come up to them, and saw what they had done, would they hesitate a moment to determine between themselves and these foolish rascals which had done wickedness? Surely not; they would immediately take hold of such stupid wicked wretches, if it was in their power, and for their brutish foolishness, have them chained in a Bedlam, or hung on a gibbet. But what would these base foolish wretches say for themselves? That they saw others do so, and they thought there had been no harm in it, and they only did as they had seen the crowd of people do before. A poor foolish, base, rascally excuse indeed! But not a better excuse than this, can the brutish enslavers and negociators of men find in all the annals of history. The ensnarers, negociators, and oppressors of men, have only to become more abandoned in wickedness than these supposed wretches could be; and to pass on in the most abominable bye paths of wickedness, and make every thing that they can see an example for their brutal barbarity; and whether it be a man hanged for his crimes, or an innocent man for the wretched wickedness of others; right or wrong it makes no difference to them, if they can only satisfy their own wretched and brutal avarice. Whether it be the Israelites subjecting the Canaanites for their crimes, or the Canaanites subjecting the Israelites, to gratify their own wickedness, it makes no difference to them. When they see some base wretches like themselves ensnaring, enslaving, oppressing, whipping, starving with hunger, and cruelly torturing and murdering some of the poor helpless part of mankind, they would think no harm in it, they would do the same. Perhaps the Greeks and Romans, and other crowds of barbarous nations have done so before; they can make that a precedent, and think no harm in it, they would still do the same, and worse than any barbarous nations ever did before: and if they look backwards and forwards they can find no better precedent, ancient or modern, than that which is wicked, mean, brutish, and base. To practise such abominable parallels of wickedness of ensnaring, negociating, and enslaving men, is the scandal and shame of mankind; And what must we think of their crimes? Let the groans and cries of the murdered, and the cruel slavery of the Africans tell!

They that can stand and look on and behold no evil in the infamous traffic of slavery must be sunk to a wonderful degree of insensibility; but surely those that can delight in that evil way for their gain, and be pleased with the wickedness of the wicked, and see no harm in subjecting their fellow-creatures to slavery, and keeping them in a state of bondage and subjection as a brute, must be wretchedly brutish indeed. But so bewitched are the general part of mankind with some sottish or selfish principle, that they care nothing about what is right or wrong, any farther than their own interest leads them to; and when avarice leads them on they can plead a thousand excuses for doing wrong, or letting others do wickedly, so as they have any advantage by it, to their own gratification and use. That sottish and selfish principle, without concern and discernment among men is such, that if they can only prosper themselves, they care nothing about the miserable situation of others: and hence it is, that even those who are elevated to high rank of power and affluence, and as becoming their eminent stations, have opportunity of extending their views afar, yet they can shut their eyes at this enormous evil of the slavery and commerce of the human species; and, contrary to all the boasted accomplishments, and fine virtues of the civilized and enlightened nations, they can sit still and let the torrent of robbery, slavery, and oppression roll on.

There is a way which seemeth good unto a man, but the end thereof are the ways of death. Should the enslavers of men think to justify themselves in their evil way, or that it can in any possible way be right for them to subject others to slavery; it is but charitable to evince and declare unto them, that they are those who have gone into that evil way of brutish stupidity as well as wickedness, that they can behold nothing of moral rectitude and equity among men but in the gloomy darkness of their own hemisphere, like the owls and night-hawks, who can see nothing but mist and darkness in the meridian blaze of day. When men forsake the paths of virtue, righteousness, justice, and mercy, and become vitiated in any evil way, all their pretended virtues, sensibility, and prudence among men, however high they may shine in their own, and of others estimation, will only appear to be but specious villainy at last. That virtue which will ever do men any good in the end, is as far from that which some men call such, as the gaudy appearance of a glow-worm in the dark is to the intrinsic value and lustre of a diamond: for if a man hath not love in his heart to his fellow-creatures, with a generous philanthropy diffused throughout his whole soul, all his other virtues are not worth a straw.

The whole law of God is founded upon love, and the two grand branches of it are these: *Thou shalt love the Lord thy God with all thy heart and with all thy soul; and thou shalt love thy neighbour as thy-*

self. And so it was when man was first created and made: they were created male and female, and pronounced to be in the image of God, and, as his representative, to have dominion over the lower creation: and their Maker, who is love, and the intellectual Father of Spirits, blessed them, and commanded them to arise in a bond of union of nature and of blood, each being a brother and a sister together, and each the lover and the loved of one another. But when they were envied and invaded by the grand enslaver of men, all their jarring incoherency arose, and those who adhered to their pernicious usurper soon became envious, hateful, and hating one another. And those who go on to injure, ensnare, oppress, and enslave their fellow-creatures, manifest their hatred to men, and maintain their own infamous dignity and vassalage, as the servants of sin and the devil: but the man that has any honour as a man scorns their ignominious dignity: the noble philanthropist looks up to his God and Father as his only sovereign; and he looks around on his fellow men as his brethren and friends; and in every situation and case, however mean and contemptible they may seem, he endeavours to do them good: and should he meet with one in the desert, whom he never saw before, he would hail him my brother! my sister! my friend! how fares it with thee? And if he can do any of them any good it would gladden every nerve of his soul.

But as there is but *one law and one manner* prescribed universally for all mankind, *for you, and for the stranger that sojourneth with you,* and wheresover they may be scattered throughout the face of the whole earth, the difference of superiority and inferiority which are found subsisting amongst them is no way incompatible with the universal law of love, honor, righteousness, and equity; so that a free, voluntary, and sociable servitude, which is the very basis of human society, either civil or religious, whereby we serve one another that we may be served, or do good that good may be done unto us, is in all things requisite and agreeable to all law and justice. But the taking away the natural liberties of men, and compelling them to any involuntary slavery, or compulsory service, is an injury and robbery contrary to all law, civilization, reason, justice, equity, and humanity: therefore when men break through the laws of God, and the rules of civilization among men, and go forth to steal, to rob, to plunder, to oppress and to enslave, and to destroy their fellow-creatures, the laws of God and man require that they should be suppressed, and deprived of their liberty, or perhaps their lives.

But justice and equity does not always reside among men, even where some considerable degree of civilization is maintained; if it had, that most infamous reservoir of public and abandoned merchandizers and enslavers of men would not have been suffered so long, nor the poor unfortunate Africans, that never would have crossed the Atlantic to rob them, would not have become their prey. But it is just as great and as heinous a transgression of the law of God to steal, kidnap, buy, sell, and enslave any one of the Africans, as it would be to ensnare any other man in the same manner, let him be who he will. And suppose that some of the African pirates had been as dextrous as the Europeans, and that they had made excursions on the coast of Great-Britain or elsewhere, and though even assisted by some of your own insiduous neighbours, for there may be some men even among you vile enough to do such a thing if they could get money by it; and that they should carry off your sons and your daughters, and your wives and friends, to a perpetual and barbarous slavery, you would certainly think that those African pirates were justly deserving of any punishment that could be put upon them. But the European pirates and merchandizers of the human species, let them belong to what nation they will, are equally as bad; and they have no better right to steal, kidnap, buy, and carry away and sell the Africans, than the Africans would have to carry away any of the Europeans in the same barbarous and unlawful manner.

But again, let us follow the European piracy to the West-Indies, or any where among Christians, and this law of the Lord Christ must stare every infidel slave-holder in the face, *And as ye would that men should do to you, do ye also to them likewise.* But there is no slave-holder would like to have himself enslaved, and to be treated as a dog, and sold like a beast; and therefore the slave-holders, and merchandizers of men, transgress this plain law, and they commit a greater violation against it, and act more contrary unto it, than it would be for a parcel of slaves to assume authority over their masters, and compel them to slavery under them; for, if that was not doing as they would wish to be done to, it would be doing, at least, as others do to them, in a way equally as much and more wrong. But our Divine Lord and *Master Christ* also teacheth men to *forgive one another their trespasses,* and that we are not to do evil because others do so, and to revenge injuries done unto us, Wherefore it is better, and more our duty, to suffer ourselves to be lashed and cruelly treated, than to take up the task of their barbarity. The just law of God requires an equal retaliation and restoration for every injury that men may do to others, to shew the greatness of the crime; but the law of forbearance, righteousness and forgiveness, forbids the retaliation to be sought after, when it would be doing as great an injury to them, without any reparation or benefit to ourselves. For what man can restore an eye that he may have deprived another of, and if even a double punishment was to pass upon him, and that he was to lose both his eyes for the crime, that would make no reparation to the other man whom he had deprived of one eye. And so, likewise, when a man is carried captive and enslaved, and maimed and cruelly treated, that would make no adequate reparation and restitution for the injuries he had received, if he was even to get the person who had ensnared him to be taken captive and treated in the same manner. What he is to seek after is a deliverance and protection for himself, and not a revenge upon others. Wherefore the honest and upright, like the just Bethlehem Joseph, cannot think of doing evil, nor require an equal retaliation for such injuries done to them, so as to revenge themselves upon others, for that which would do them no manner of good, Such vengeance belongeth unto the Lord, and he will render vengeance and recompence to his enemies and the violaters of his law.

But thus saith the law of God: *If a man be found stealing any of his neighbours, or he that stealeth a man (let him be who he will) and selleth him, or that maketh merchandize of him, or if he be found in his hand, then that thief shall die.* However, in all modern slavery among Christians, who ought to know this law, they have not had any regard to it. Surely if any law among them admits of death as a punishment for robbing or defrauding others of their money or goods, it ought to be double death, if it was possible, when a man is robbed of himself, and sold into captivity and cruel slavery. But because of his own goodness, and because of the universal depravity of men, the Sovereign Judge of all has introduced a law of forbearance, to spare such transgressors, where in many cases the law denounces death as the punishment for their crimes, unless for those founded upon murder, or such abominations as cannot be forborn with in any civilization among men. But this law of forbearance is no alteration of the law itself; it is only a respite in order to spare such as will fly to him for refuge and forgiveness for all their crimes, and for all their iniquities, who is the righteous fulfiller of the law, and the surety and representative of men before God: and if they do not repent of their iniquity, and reform to a life of new obedience, as being under greater obligations to the law, but go on in their evil way, they must at last for ever lie under the curse and every penalty of the just and holy law of that Most High. This seems to be determined so by that Great Judge of the law, when the accusers of a woman, taken in adultery, brought her before him, he stooped down as a man and wrote, we may suppose, the crimes of her accusers in the dust, and as the God of all intelligence painted them in their consciences, wherefore they fled away one by one, and the woman was left alone before him; and as there was none of her accusers in that case righteous enough to throw the first stone, and to execute the law upon her, she was, Bid to go and sin no more. But it is manifest that every crime that men may commit, where death is mentioned as the penalty thereof in the righteous law of God, it denotes a very great offence and a heinous trangression; and although, in many cases, it may meet with some mitigation in the punishment, because of the forbearance of God, and the unrighteousness of men, it cannot thereby be thought the less criminal in itself. But it also supposes, where strict severities are made use of in the laws of civilization, that the doers of the law, and the judges of it, ought to be very righteous themselves. And with regard to that law of men-stealers, merchandizers, and of slaves found in their hands, that whatever mitigation and forbearance such offenders ought to meet with, their crimes denote a very heinous offence, and a great violation of the law of God; they ought, therefore, to be punished according to their trespasses, which, in some cases, should be death, if the person so robbed and stole should die in consequence thereof, or should not be restored and brought back; and even then to be liable to every damage and penalty that the judges should think proper: for so it is annexed to this law and required, that men should put away evil from among them. But this cannot now extend to the West-India slavery: what should rather be required of them, in their present case of infatuation, is to surrender and give it up, and heal the stripes that they have wounded, and to pour the healing balm of Christianity into the bleeding wounds of Heathen barbarity and cruelty.

All the criminal laws of civilization seem to be founded upon that law of God which was published to Noah and his sons; and, consequently, as it is again and again repeated, it becomes irreversible, and universal to all mankind. *And surely your blood of your lives will I require: at the hand of every beast will I require it; and at the hand of man, at the hand of every man's brother, will I require the life of man. Whoso sheddeth man's blood, by man shall his blood be shed: for in the image of God made he man.* If this law of God had not been given to men, murder itself would not, have been any crime; and those who punished it with death would just have been as guilty as the other. But the law of God is just, righteous and holy, and ought to be regarded and revered above all the laws of men; and this is added unto it: *What thing soever I command you, observe to do it: thou shalt not add thereto, nor diminish from it.* But it is an exceeding impious thing for men ever to presume, or think, as some will say, that they would make it death as a punishment for such a thing, and such a trespass; or that they can make any criminal laws of civilization as binding with a penalty of death for any thing just what they please. No such thing can be supposed; no man upon earth ever had, or ever can have, a right to make laws where a penalty of cutting off by death is required as the punishment for the transgression thereof: what is required of men is to be the doers of the law, and some of them to be judges of it; and if they judge wrongfully in taking away the lives of their fellow-creatures contrary to the law of God, they commit murder.

The reason why a man suffers death for breaking the laws of his country is, because he transgresseth the law of God in that community he belongs to; and the laws of civilization are binding to put that law in force, and to point out and shew a sufficient warrant wherefore he should suffer, according as the just law of God requires for his trespass; and then it is just and right that he should die for his crime. And as murder is irreversibly to be punished with death, sometimes when it is not done, but only implied or eventually intended, it even then requires death; and in this sense it becomes right to face our enemies in the field of battle, and to cut them off. And when spies and incendiaries rise up, or when rebellions break forth, and the lives of the Sovereign and others, and the good of the community is not safe while such pretenders and their chief supporters are suffered to live; then it may be lawful, in some cases, that they should die; but in cases of this kind there is generally more cowardice and cruelty than justice and mercy regarded, and more discretionary power left for men to use their authority in, and to establish criminal laws or precedents than in any thing else. Hence we may find many of the different chiefs and kings in different parts of the world, in all ages, wading through a sea of blood to their thrones, or supporting themselves upon it, by desolating and destroying others; and we may find good and bad in all ages setting up wretched examples for men to be guided by; and herein we may find a

David, a Solomon, a Cromwell, committing murder and death, and a
Charles the Second committing a greater carnage upon more innocent
people than those who suffered in the reign of a bloody Queen Mary;
and even in a late rebellion there were many suffered in Britain, which,
if they had been preserved to this mild reign, they would have been
as good neighbours, and as faithful subjects, as any other. But among
all pretences for taking away the lives of men by any form of law, that
for religion is the most unwarrantable: it is the command of God to
suppress idolatry, and to break down the images and external pomp of
gross superstition, but not to destroy men themselves: that persecution
is murder if it takes away the lives of men for their religion, for it has
nothing to do with what men may think with respect to their own
duty; and if a man is foolish enough to make an image of wood or
stone, and to worship it, or even to adore a picture, if he keeps it to
himself, persecution has nothing to do with him.

The law of God forbids all manner of covetousness and theft: but
when any thing is taken away by stealth, it is not like those injuries
which cannot be restored, as the cutting off or wounding any of the
members of the body; but it admits of a possible restoration, whether
the violators can restore it or not as the law requires, so if a man owes
a just debt it is not the less due by him if he has got nothing to pay it
with; such trangressors ought to be punished according to their trespasses, but not with death: for the law of God is, "If a thief be found
breaking up, and he be smitten that he die, if it was in the night there
shall be no blood shed for him; but if the sun be risen upon him, there
was blood required for him if he was killed; for saith the law it required
only he should make full restitution; and if he had nothing, then he
should be sold for his theft. And if any manner of theft be found in
a man's hand, the law requires a retaliation and restoration; that is,
that he should restore double; but if it be sold or made away with, it
was then to be fourfold, and, in some cases, five, six or seven times
as much*." According to this law, when the property of others is tak-
en away, either by stealth, fraud, or violence, the aggressors should be
subjected to such bondage and hard labour, (and especially when the
trespass is great, and they have nothing to pay) as would be requisite
to make restitution to the injured, and to bring about a reformation

---

* A great part of this law is strictly observed in Africa, and we make use
of sacrifices, and keep a Sabbath every seventh day, more strictly than
Christians generally do.

to themselves. And if they have committed violence either by threats or force, they ought to suffer bodily punishment, and the severity of it according to their crimes, and the stubbornness of their obduracy; and all such punishments as are necessary should be inflicted upon them without pitying or sparing them, though perhaps not to be continued for ever in the brutal manner that the West-India slaves suffer for almost no crimes.

But whereas the robbing of others in any manner of their property is often attended with such cruelty and violence, and a severe loss to the sufferers, it may, in some cases, be thought that the law of God sufficiently warrants the taking away the lives of the aggressors; for the taking away of a man's property in general may be considered as taking away his life, or at least the means of his support, and then the punishing the transgressors with death can only in that case be reckoned a constructive murder. Wherefore the transgressors ought to be punished severely; but never with any laws of civilization where death is concerned, without a regard to the law of God. And when the law of God admits of a forbearance, and a kind of forgiveness in many things, it ought to be the grand law of civilization to seek out such rules of punishment as are best calculated to prevent injuries of every kind, and to reclaim the transgressors; and it is best, if it can be done, to punish with a less degree of severity than their crimes deserve. But all the laws of civilization must jar greatly when the law of God is screwed up in the greatest severity to punish men for their crimes on the one hand, and on the other to be totally disregarded*. When the Divine law points out a theft, where the thief should make restitution for his trespass, the laws of civilization say, he must die for his crime: and when that law tells us, that he who stealeth or maketh merchandize of men, that such a thief shall surely die, the laws of civilization say, in many cases, that it is no crime. In this the ways of men are not equal; but let the wise and just determine whether the laws of God or the laws of men are right.

Amongst some of the greatest transgressors of the laws of civilization, those that defraud the public by forgery, or by substituting or falsifying any of the current specie, ought to have their lives or their liberties taken away; for although they may not do any personal injury,

---

* This confessional minstrel may often be repeated, but, I fear, seldom regarded: "We have offended against thy holy laws; we have left undone those things which we ought to have done; and we have done those things which we ought not to have done."

they commit the greatest robbery and theft, both to individuals and the whole community. But even in the suppression of those, men have no right to add or diminsh any thing to the law of God, with respect to taking away their lives. Wherefore, if the law of God does not so clearly warrant, that they should die for their theft, it, at least, fully warrants that they should be sold into slavery for their crimes; and the laws of civilization may justly bind them, and hold them in perpetual bondage, because they have sold themselves to work iniquity; but not that they should be sold to the heathen, or to such as would not instruct them: for there might be hope, that if good instruction was properly administered unto them, there might be a possible reformation wrought upon some of them. Some, by their ingenious assiduity, have tamed the most savage wild beasts; it is certainly more laudable to tame the most brutish and savage men, and, in time, there might be some Onesimus's found amongst them, that would become useful to reclaim others. Those that break the laws of civilization, in any flagrant manner, are the only species of men that others have a right to enslave; and such ought to be sold to the community, with every thing that can be found belonging to them, to make a commutation of restitution as far as could be; and they should be kept at some useful and laborious employment, and it might be at some embankation, or recovering of waste ground, as there might be land recovered on rivers and shores, worth all the expence, for the benefit of the community they belonged to. The continuance of that criminal slavery and bondage, ought to be according to the nature of their crimes, with a reference to their good behaviour, either to be continued or protracted. Such as were condemned for life, when their crimes were great, and themselves stubborn, might be so marked as to render their getting away impossible without being discovered, and that the very sight of one of them might deter others from committing their crimes, as much as hanging perhaps a dozen of them; and it might be made so severe unto them, that it would render their own society in bondage, almost the only preferable one that they could enjoy among men. The manner of confining them would not be so impracticable as some may be apt to think; and all these severities come under the laws of men to punish others for their crimes, but they should not go beyond the just law of God; and neither should his laws be suspended, where greater trespasses are committed.

In this sense every free community might keep slaves, or criminal prisoners in bondage; and should they be sold to any other, it should not be to strangers, nor without their own consent; and if any were sold for a term of years, they would naturally become free as soon as their purchase could be paid. But if any man should buy another man without his own consent, and compel him to his service and slavery without any agreement of that man to serve him, the enslaver is a robber, and a defrauder of that man every day. Wherefore it is as much the duty of a man who is robbed in that manner to get out of the hands of his enslaver, as it is for any honest community of men to get out of the hands of rogues and villains. And however much is required of men to forgive one another their trespasses in one respect, it is also manifest, and what we are commanded, as noble, to resist evil in another, in order to prevent others doing evil, and to keep ourselves from harm. Therefore, if there was no other way to deliver a man from slavery, but by enslaving his master, it would be lawful for him to do so if he was able, for this would be doing justice to himself, and be justice, as the law requires, to chastise his master for enslaving of him wrongfully.

Thence this general and grand duty should be observed by every man, not to follow the multitude to do evil, neither to recompence evil for evil; and yet, so that a man may lawfully defend himself, and endeavour to secure himself, and others, as far as he can, from injuries of every kind. Wherefore all along, in the history of mankind, the various depredations committed in the world, by enslaving, extirpating and destroying men, were always contrary to the laws of God, and what he had strictly forbidden and commanded not to be done. But insolent, proud, wicked men, in all ages, and in all places, are alike; they disregard the laws of the Most High, and stop at no evil in their power, that they can contrive with any pretence of consistency in doing mischief to others, so as it may tend to promote their own profit and ambition. Such are all the depredators, kidnappers, merchandizers and enslavers of men; they do not care, nor consider, how much they injure others, if they can make any advantage to themselves by it. But whenever these things were committed by wicked men, a retaliation was sought after, as the only way of deliverance; for he who leadeth into captivity, should be carried captive; and he which destroyeth with the sword, should die with the sword. And as it became necessary to punish those that wronged others, when the punishers went beyond the bounds of a just retaliation, and fell into the same crimes of the oppressors, not to prevent themselves from harm, and to deliver the oppressed and the captive, but to oppress and enslave others, as much as they before them had done, the consequence is plain, that an impending overthrow must still fall upon them likewise. In that respect, so far as conquerors are permitted to become a judgment and a scourge to others, for their enormous transgressions, they are themselves not a bit the more safe, for what they do, they often do wickedly for their own purpose; and when the purpose of Divine Providence, who raised them up, is fulfilled by them, in the punishment of others for their crimes; the next wave thereof will be to visit them also according to their wickedness with some dreadful overthrow, and to swallow them up in the sea of destruction and oblivion.

History affords us many examples of severe retaliations, revolutions and dreadful overthrows; and of many crying under the heavy load of subjection and oppression, seeking for deliverance. And methinks I hear now, many of my countrymen, in complexion, crying and groaning under the heavy yoke of slavery and bondage, and praying to be delivered; and the word of the Lord is thus speaking for them, while they are bemoaning themselves under the grievous bonds of their misery and woe, saying, *Woe is me*! alas Africa! *for I am as the last gleanings of the summer fruit, as the grape gleanings of the vintage, where no cluster is to eat. The good are perished out of the earth, and there is none upright among men; they all lie in wait for blood; they hunt every man his brother with a net. That they may do evil with both hands earnestly, the prince asketh, and the judge asketh for a reward; and the great man he uttereth his mischievous desire: so they wrap it up.* Among the best in Africa, we have found them sharp as a briar; among the most upright, we have found them sharper than a thorn-hedge in the West-Indies. Yet, O Africa! yet, poor slave! *The day of thy watchmen cometh, and thy visitation draweth nigh, that shall be their perplexity. Therefore I will look unto the Lord; I will wait for the God of my salvation; my God will hear me. Rejoice not against me, O mine enemy; though I be fallen, I shall yet arise; though I sit in darkness, the Lord shall yet be a light unto me. I will bear the indignation of the Lord, because I have sinned against him, until he plead my cause, and execute judgment for me, and I shall behold his righteousness. Then mine enemies shall see it, and shame shall cover them which said unto me, Where is the Lord thy God*, that regardeth thee: *Mine eyes shall behold them trodden down as the mire of the streets. In that day that thy walls of deliverance are to be built, in that day shall the decree of slavery be far removed.*

What revolution the end of that predominant evil of slavery and oppression may produce, whether the wise and considerate will surrender and give it up, and make restitution for the injuries that they have already done, as far as they can; or whether the force of their wickedness, and the iniquity of their power, will lead them on until some universal calamity burst forth against the abandoned carriers of it on, and against the criminal nations in confederacy with them, is not for me to determine? But this must appear evident, that for any man to carry on a traffic in the merchandize of slaves, and to keep them in slavery; or for any nation to oppress, extirpate and destroy others; that these are crimes of the greatest magnitude, and a most daring violation of the laws and commandments of the Most High, and which, at last, will be evidenced in the destruction and overthrow of all the transgressors. And nothing else can be expected for such violations of taking away the natural rights and liberties of men, but that those who are the doers of it will meet with some awful visitation of the righteous judgment of God, and in such a manner as it cannot be thought that his just vengeance for their iniquity will be the less tremendous because his judgments are long delayed.

None but men of the most brutish and depraved nature, led on by the invidious influence of infernal wickedness, could have made their settlements in the different parts of the world discovered by them, and have treated the various Indian nations, in the manner that the barbarous inhuman Europeans have done: and their establishing and carrying on that most dishonest, unjust and diabolical traffic of buying and selling, and of enslaving men, is such a monstrous, audacious and unparallelled wickedness, that the very idea of it is shocking, and the whole nature of it is horrible and infernal. It may be said with confidence as a certain general fact, that all their foreign settlements and colonies were founded on murders and devastations, and that they have continued their depredations in cruel slavery and oppression to this day: for where such predominant wickedness as the African slave-trade, and the West Indian slavery, is admitted, tolerated and supported by them, and carried on in their colonies, the nations and people who are the supporters and encouragers thereof must be not only guilty themselves of that shameful and abandoned evil and wickedness, so very disgraceful to human nature, but even partakers in those crimes of the most vile combinations of various pirates, kidnappers, robbers and thieves, the ruffians and stealers of men, that ever made their appearance in the world.

Soon after Columbus had discovered America, that great navigator was himself greatly embarrassed and treated unjustly, and his best designs counteracted by the wicked baseness of those whom he led to that discovery. The infernal conduct of his Spanish competitors, whose leading motives were covetousness, avarice and fanaticism, soon made their appearance, and became cruel and dreadful. At Hispaniola the base perfidy and bloody treachery of the Spaniards, led on by the perfidious Ovando, in seizing the peaceable Queen Anacoana and her attendants, burning her palace, putting all to destruction, and the innocent Queen and her people to a cruel death, is truly horrible and lamentable. And led on by the treacherous Cortes, the fate of the great Montezuma was dreadful and shocking; how that American monarch was treated, betrayed and destroyed, and his vast extensive empire of the Mexicans brought to ruin and devastation, no man of sensibility and feeling can read the history without pity and resentment. And looking over another page of that history, sensibility would kindle into horror and indignation, to see the base treacherous bastard Pizarra at the head of the Spanish banditti of miscreant depredators, leading them on, and overturning one of the most extensive empires in the world. To recite a little of this as a specimen of the rest: It seems Pizarra, with his company of depredators, had artfully penetrated into the Peruvian empire, and pretended an embassy of peace from a great monarch, and demanded an audience of the noble Atahualpa, the great Inca or Lord of that empire, that the terms of their embassy might be explained, and the reason of their coming into the territories of that monarch. Atahualpa fearing the menaces of those terrible invaders, and thinking to appease them by complying with their request, relied on Pizarra's feigned pretensions of friendship; accordingly the day was appointed, and Atahualpa made his appearance with the greatest decency and splendor he could, to meet such superior beings as the Americans conceived their invaders to be, with four hundred men in an uniform dress, as harbingers to clear the way before him, and himself sitting on a throne or couch, adorned with plumes of various colours, and almost covered with plates of gold and silver, enriched with precious stones, and was carried on the shoulders of his principal attendants. As he approached near the Spanish quarters the arch fanatic Father Vincent Valverde, chaplain to the expedition, advanced with a crucifix in one hand and a breviary in the other, and began with a long discourse, pretending to explain some of the general doctrines of Christianity, together with the fabulous notion of St. Peter's vicegerency, and the transmission of his apostolic power continued in the succession of the Popes; and that the then Pope, Alexander, by donation, had invested their master as the sole Monarch of all the New World. In consequence of this, Atahualpa was instantly required to embrace the Christian religion, acknowledge the jurisdiction of the Pope, and submit to the Great Monarch of Castile; but if he should refuse an immediate compliance with these requisitions, they were to declare war against him, and that he might expect the dreadful effects of their vengeance. This strange harangue, unfolding deep mysteries, and alluding to such unknown facts, of which no power of eloquence could translate, and convey, at once, a distinct idea to an American, that its general tenor was altogether incomprehensible to Atahualpa. Some parts in it, as more obvious than the rest, filled him with astonishment and indignation. His reply, however, was temperate, and as suitable as could be well expected. He observed that he was Lord of the dominions over which he reigned by hereditary succession; and, said, that he could not conceive how a foreign priest should pretend to dispose of territories which did not belong to him, and that if such a preposterous grant had been made, he, who was the rightful possessor, refused to confirm it; that he had no inclination to renounce the religious institutions established by his ancestors; nor would he forsake the service of the Sun, the immortal divinity whom he and his people revered, in order to worship the God of the Spaniards, who was subject to death; and that with respect to other matters, he had never heard of them before, and did not then understand their meaning. And he desired to know where Valverde had learned things so extraordinary. In this book, replied the fanatic Monk, reaching out his breviary. The Inca opened it eagerly, and turning over the leaves, lifted it to his ear: This, says he, is silent; it tell tells me nothing; and threw it with disdain to the ground. The enraged father of ruffians, turning towards his countrymen, the assassinators, cried out, To arms, Christians, to arms; the word of God is insulted; avenge this profanation on these impious dogs.

At this the Christian desperadoes impatient in delay, as soon as the signal of assault was given their martial music began to play, and their attack was rapid, rushing suddenly upon the Peruvians, and with their hell-invented enginery of thunder, fire and smoke, they soon put them to flight and destruction. The Inca, though his nobles crouded round him with officious zeal, and fell in numbers at his feet, while they vied one with another in sacrificing their own lives that they might cover the sacred person of their Sovereign, was soon penetrated to by the assassinators, dragged from his throne, and carried to the Spanish quarters. The fate of the Monarch increased the precipitate flight of his followers; the plains being covered with upwards of thirty thousand men, were pursued by the ferocious Spaniards towards every quarter, who, with deliberate and unrelenting barbarity, continued to slaughter the wretched fugitives till the close of the day, that never had once offered at any resistance. Pizarra had contrived this daring and perfidious plan on purpose to get hold of the Inca, notwithstanding his assumed character of an ambassador from a powerful monarch to court an alliance with that prince, and in violation of all the repeated offers of his own friendship. The noble Inca thus found himself betrayed and shut up in the Spanish quarters, though scarce aware at first of the vast carnage and destruction of his people; but soon conceiving the destructive consequences that attended his confinement, and by beholding the vast treasures of spoil that the Spaniards had so eagerly gathered up, he learned something of their covetous disposition: and he offered as a ransom what astonished the Spaniards, even after all they now knew concerning the opulence of his kingdom: the apartment in which he was confined was twenty-two feet in length and sixteen in breadth, he undertook to fill it with vessels of gold as high as he could reach. This tempting proposal was eagerly agreed to by Pizarra, and a line was drawn upon the walls of the chamber to mark the stipulated height to which the treasure was to rise. The gold was accordingly collected from various parts with the greatest expedition by the Inca's obedient and loving subjects, who thought nothing too much for his ransom and life; but, after all, poor Atahualpa was cruelly murdered, and his body burnt by a military inquisition, and his extensive and rich dominions devoted to destruction and ruin by these merciless depredators.

The history of those dreadfully perfidious methods of forming settlements, and acquiring riches and territory, would make humanity tremble, and even recoil, at the enjoyment of such acquisitions and become reverted into rage and indignation at such horrible injustice and barbarous cruelty, "It is said by the Peruvians, that their Incas, or Monarchs, had uniformly extended their power with attention to the good of their subjects, that they might diffuse the blessings of civilization, and the knowledge of the arts which they possessed, among the people that embraced their protection; and during a succession of twelve monarchs, not one had deviated from this beneficent character." Their sensibility of such nobleness of character would give them the most poignant dislike to their new terrible invaders that had desolated and laid waste their country. The character of their monarchs would seeem to vie with as great virtues as any King in Europe can boast of. Had the Peruvians been visited by men of honesty, knowledge, and enlightened understanding, to teach them, by patient instruction and the blessing of God, they might have been induced to embrace the doctrines and faith of Christianity, and to abandon their errors of superstition and idolatry. Had Christians, that deserve the name thereof, been sent among them, the many useful things that they would have taught them, together with their own pious example, would have captivated their hearts; and the knowledge of the truth would have made it a very desirous thing for the Americans to have those that taught them to settle among them. Had that been the case the Americans, in various parts, would have been as eager to have the Europeans to come there as they would have been to go, so that the Europeans might have found settlements enough, in a friendly alliance with the inhabitants, without destroying and enslaving them. And had that been the case, it might be supposed, that Europe and America, long before now, would both, with a growing luxuriancy, have been flourishing with affluence and peace, and their long extended and fruitful branches, loaden with benefits to each other, reaching over the ocean, might have been more extensive, and greater advantages have been expected, for the good of both than what has yet appeared. But, alas! at that time there was no Christians to send,) and very few now), these were obliged to hide themselves in the obscure places of the earth; that was, according to Sir Isaac Newton, to mix in obscurity among the meanest of the people, having no power and authority; and it seems at that time there was no power among Christians on earth to have sent such as would have been useful to the Americans; if there had they would have sent after the depredators, and rescued the innocent.

But as I said before, it is surely to the great shame and scandal of Christianity among all the Heathen nations, that those robbers, plunderers, destroyers and enslavers of men should call themselves Christians, and exercise their power under any Christian government and authority. I would have my African countrymen to know and un-

derstand, that the destroyers and enslavers of men can be no Christians; for Christianity is the system of benignity and love, and all its
votaries are devoted to honesty, justice, humanity, meekness, peace and
good-will to all men. But whatever title or claim some may assume to
call themselves by it, without possessing any of its virtues, can only
manifest them to be the more abominable liars, and the greatest enemies unto it, and as belonging to the synagogue of Satan, and not the
adherers to Christ. For the enslavers and oppressors of men, among
those that have obtained the name of Christians, they are still acting
as its greatest enemies, and contrary to all its genuine principles; they
should therefore be called by its opposite, the Antichrist. Such are fitly
belonging to that most dissolute sorceress of all religion in the world:
"With whom the kings of the earth have lived deliciously; and the
inhabitants of the earth have been made drunk with the wine of her
abominations; and the merchants of the earth are waxed rich through
the abundance of her delicacies, by their traffic in various things, and
in slaves and souls of men!" It was not enough for the malignant de-
stroyer of the world to set up his hydra-headed kingdom of evil and
wickedness among the kingdom of men; but also to cause an image to
be made unto him, by something imported in the only true religion
that ever was given to men; and that image of iniquity is described as
arising up out of the earth, having two horns like a lamb, which, by
its votaries and adherents, has been long established and supported.
One of its umbragious horns of apostacy and delusion is founded, in
a more particular respect, on a grand perversion of the Old Testament
dispensations, which has extended itself over all the Mahometan nations in the East; and the other horn of apostacy, bearing an allusion
and professional respect to that of the new, has extended itself over all
the Christian nations in the West. That grand umbragious shadow and
image of evil and wickedness, has spread its malignant influence over
all the nations of the earth, and has, by its power of delusion, given
countenance and support to all the power of evil and wickedness done
among men; and all the adherents and supporters of that delusion,
and all the carriers on of wickedness, are fitly called Antichrist. But
all the nations have drunk of the wine of that iniquity, and become
drunk with the wine of the wrath of her fornication, whose name, by
every mark and feature, is the Antichrist; and every dealer in slaves and
those that hold them in slavery, whatever else they may call themselves,
or whatever else they may profess. And likewise, those nations whose

governments support that evil and wicked traffic of slavery, however remote the situation where it is carried on may be, are, in that respect, as much Antichristian as any thing in the world can be. No man will ever rob another unless he be a villain: nor will any nation or people ever enslave and oppress others, unless themselves be base and wicked men, and who act and do contrary and against every duty in Christianity.

The learned and ingenious author of Britannia Libera, as chiefly alluding to Great Britain alone, gives some account of that great evil and wickedness carried on by the Christian nations, respecting the direful effects of the great devastations committed in foreign parts, whereby it would appear that the ancient and native inhabitants have been drenched in blood and oppression by their merciless visitors (which have formed colonies and settlements among them) the avaricious depredators, plunderers and destroyers of nations. As some estimate of it, "to destroy eleven million, and distress many more in America, to starve and oppress twelve million in Asia, and the great number destroyed, is not the way to promote the dignity, strength and safety of empire, but to draw down the Divine vengeance on the offenders, for depriving so many of their fellow-creatures of life, or the common blessings of the earth: whereas by observing the humane principles of preservation with felicitation, the proper principles of all rulers, their empire might have received all reasonable benefit, with the encrease of future glory." But should it be asked, what advantages Great-Britain has gained by all its extensive territories abroad, the devastations committed, and the abominable slavery and oppression carried on in its colonies? It may be answered according to the old proverb,

It seldom is the grand-child's lot,
To share of wealth unjustly got.

This seems to be verified too much in their present situation: for however wide they have extended their territories abroad, they have sunk into a world of debt at home, which must ever remain an impending burden upon the inhabitants. And it is not likely, by any plan as yet adopted, to be ever paid, or any part of it, without a long continued heavy annual load of taxes. Perhaps, great as it is some other plan, more equitable for the good of the whole community, if it was wanted to be done, and without any additional taxes, might be so made use of to pay it all off in twenty or thirty years time, and in such manner as whatever emergencies might happen, as never to need to borrow any money at interest. The national debt casts a sluggish deadness over the whole realm, greatly stops ingenuity and improvements, promotes idleness and wickedness, clogs all the wheels of commerce, and drains the money out of the nation. If a foreigner buys stock, in the course of years that the interest amounts to the principal, he gets it all back; and in an equitable time the same sum ever after, and in course must take that money to foreign parts. And those who hold stock at home, are a kind of idle drones, as a burden to the rest of the community: whereas if there were no funds, those who have money would be obliged to occupy it in some improvements themselves, or lend it to other manufacturers or merchants, and by that means useful employments, ingenuity and commerce would flourish. But all stock-jobbing, lotteries, and useless business, has a tendency to slavery and oppression; for as the greater any idle part of the community is, there must be the greater labour and hardships resting upon the industrious part who support the rest; as all men are allotted in some degree to eat their bread with the sweat of their brow; *but it is evil with any people when the rich grind the face of the poor.* Lotteries must be nearly as bad a way of getting money for the good of a nation, as it is for an individual when he is poor, and obliged to pawn his goods to increase his poverty, already poor. On the reverse, if a nation was to keep a bank to lend money to merchants and others, that nation might flourish, and its support to those in need might be attended with advantage to the whole; but that nation which is obliged to borrow money from others, must be in a poor and wretched situation, and the inhabitants, who have to bear the load of its taxes, must be greatly burdened, and perhaps many of those employed in its service (as soldiers and others) poorly paid. It was otherwise with *the people of Israel of old*; it was the premise and blessing of God to them, *That they should lend unto many nations, but should not borrow.*

But when a nation or people do wickedly, and commit cruelties and devastations upon others, and enslave them, it cannot be expected that they should be attended with the blessings of God, neither to eschew evil. They often become infatuated to do evil unawares; and those employed under their service sometimes lead them into debt, error and wickedness, in order to enrich themselves by their plunder, in committing the most barbarous cruelties, under pretences of war, wherein they were the first aggressors, and which is generally the case in all unnatural and destructive disputes of war. In this business money is wanted, the national debt becomes increased, and new loans and other sums must be added to the funds. The plunderers abroad send home their cash as fast as they can, and by one means and another the sums wanted to borrow, are soon made up. At last when the wars subside, or other business calls them home, laden with the spoils of the East or elsewhere, they have then the grand part of their business to negociate, in buying up bank stock, and lodging their plunder and ill-got wealth in the British or other funds. Thus the nation is loaded with more debt, and with an annual addition of more interest to pay, to the further advantage of those who often occasioned it by their villainy; who, if they had their deserts, like the Popish inquisitors, are almost the only people in the world who deserve to be hung on the rack.

But so it happens in general, that men of activity and affluence, by whatever way they are possessed of riches, or have acquired a greatness of such property, they are always preferred to take the lead in matters of government, so that the greatest depredators, warriors, contracting companies of merchants, and rich slave-holders, always endeavour to push themselves on to get power and interest in their favour; that whatever crimes any of them commit they are seldom brought to a just punishment. Unless that something of this kind had been the case, 'tis impossible to conceive how such an enormous evil as the slave-trade could have been established and carried on under any Christian government: and from hence that motly system of government, which hath so sprung up and established itself, may be accounted for, and as being an evident and universal depravity of one of the finest constitutions in the world; and it may be feared if these unconstitutional laws reaching from Great-Britain to her colonies, be long continued in and supported, to the carrying on that horrible and wicked traffic of slavery, must at last mark out the whole of the British constitution with ruin and destruction; and that the most generous and tenacious people in the world for liberty, may also at last be reduced to slaves. And an Ethiopian may venture to assert, that so long as slavery is continued in any part of the British dominions, that more than one-half of the legislature are the virtual supporters and encouragers of a traffic which ought to be abolished, as it cannot be carried on but by some of the most abandoned and profligate men upon earth.

However, the partizans of such a class of men are generally too many and numerous, whose viciated principles from time to time have led the whole nation into debt, error and disgrace; and by their magnetic influence there is a general support given to despotism, oppression and cruelty. For many have acquired great riches by some insidious traffic or illegal gain; and as these become often leading men in governments, vast multitudes by sea and land pursue the same course, and support the same measures; like adventurers in the lottery, each grasping for the highest prize; or as much enamoured with any infamous way of getting riches, as the Spaniards were with the Peruvian vessels of gold. And when ambitious and wicked men are bent upon avarice and covetousness, it leads them on to commit terrible cruelties, and their hearts become hardened in wickedness; so that even their enormous crimes sink in their own estimation, and soften into trivial matters. The house-breakers and highwaymen, petty depredators, think nothing of any mischief or cruelty that they can do, so as they can gain their end and come off safe; but their villainy and crimes appear to other men as they ought to do, and if they can be detected, and taken hold of, they will meet with such punishment as they justly deserve for their crimes. But it is otherwise with the Colonians, the great depredators, pirates, kidnappers, robbers, oppressors and enslavers of men. The laws as reaching from Great-Britain to the West-Indies, do not detect them, but protect the opulent slave-holders; though their opulence and protection by any law, or any government whatsoever, cannot make them less criminal than violators of the common rights and liberties of men. They do not take away a man's property, like other robbers; but they take a man himself, and subject him to their service and bondage, which is a greater robbery, and a greater crime, than taking away any property from men whatsoever. And, therefore, with respect to them, there is very much wanted for regulating the natural rights of mankind, and very much wrong in the present forms of government, as well as much abuse of that which is right.

The Spaniards began their settlements in the West Indies and America, by depredations of rapine, injustice, treachery and murder; and they have continued in the barbarous practice of devastation, cruelty, and oppression ever since: and their principles and maxims in planting colonies have been adopted, in some measure, by every other nation in Europe. This guiltful method of colonization must undoubtedly and imperceptibly have hardened men's hearts, and led them on from one degree of barbarity and cruelty to another: for when they had destroyed, wasted and desolated the native inhabitants, and when many of their own people, enriched with plunder, had retired, or returned home to enjoy their ill-gotten wealth, other resources for men to labour and cultivate the ground, and such other laborious employ-

ments were wanted. Vast territories and large possessions, without getting inhabitants to labour for them, were of no use. A general part of
what remained of the wretched fugitives, who had the best native right
to those possessions, were obliged to make their escape to places more
remote, and such as could not, were obliged to submit to the hard
labour and bondage of their invaders; but as they had not been used
to such harsh treatment and laborious employment as they were then
subjected to, they were soon wasted away and became few. Their proud
invaders found the advantage of having their labour done for nothing,
and it became their general practice to pick up the unfortunate strangers that fell in their way, when they thought they could make use of
them in their service. That base traffic of kidnapping and stealing men
was begun by the Portuguese on the coast of Africa, and as they found
the benefit of it for their own wicked purposes, they soon went on to
commit greater depredations. The Spaniards followed their infamous
example, and the African slave-trade was thought most advantageous
for them, to enable themselves to live in ease and affluence by the cruel
subjection and slavery of others. The French and English, and some
other nations in Europe, as they founded settlements and colonies in
the West-Indies. Or in America, went on in the same manner, and
joined hand in hand with the Portuguese and Spaniards, to rob and
pillage Africa, as well as to waste and desolate the inhabitants of the
western continent. But the European depredators and pirates have not
only robbed and pillaged the people of Africa themselves; but, by their
instigation, they have infested the inhabitants with some of the vilest
combinations of fraudulent and treacherous villains, even among their
own people; and have set up their forts and factories as a reservoir of
public and abandoned thieves, and as a den of desperadoes, where they
may ensnare, entrap and catch men. So that Africa has been robbed of
its inhabitants; its free-born sons and daughters have been stole, and
kidnapped, and violently taken away, and carried into captivity and
cruel bondage. And it may be said, in respect to that diabolical traffic
which is still carried on by the European depredators, that Africa has
suffered as much and more than any other quarter of the globe. O merciful God! when will the wickedness of man have an end?

The Royal African Company (as it is called, ought rather to be reversed as unworthy of the name) was incorporated 14th Charles II. and
impowered to trade from Salle in South Barbary to the Cape of Good
Hope, and to erect forts and factories on the western coast of Africa

for that purpose. But this trade was laid open by an act of parliament, Anno 1697, and every private merchant permitted to trade thither, upon paying the sum of ten pounds towards maintaining the forts and garrisons. This Company, for securing their commerce, erected several factories on the coast; the most remarkable are these, viz. on the North part of Guinea, James Fort, upon an island in the River Gambia, Sierra Leona, and Sherbro; and on the South part of Guinea, viz. on the Gold Coast, Dick's Cove, Succunda, Commenda, Cape Coast Castle, Fort Royal, Queen Anne's Point, Charles Fort, Annamabo, Winebah, Shidoe, Acra, &c. In all these places it is their grand business to traffic in the human species; and dreadful and shocking as it is to think, it has even been established by royal authority, and is still supported and carried on under a Christian government; and this must evidently appear thereby, that the learned, the civilized, and even the enlightened nations are become as truly barbarous and brutish as the unlearned.

To give any just conception of the barbarous traffic carried on at those factories, it would be out of my power to describe the miserable situation of the poor exiled Africans, which by the craft of wicked men daily become their prey, though I have seen enough of their misery as well as read; no description can give an adequate idea of the horror of their feelings, and the dreadful calamities they undergo. The treacherous, perfidious and cruel methods made use of in procuring them, are horrible and shocking. The bringing them to the ships and factories, and subjecting them to brutal examinations stripped naked and markings, is barbarous and base. The stowing them in the holds of the ships like goods of burden, with closeness and stench, is deplorable; and, what makes addition to this deplorable situation, they are often treated in the most barbarous and inhuman manner by the unfeeling monsters of Captains. And when they arrive at the destined port in the colonies, they are again stripped naked for the brutal examination of their purchasers to view them, which, to many, must add shame and grief to their other woe, as may be evidently seen with sorrow, melancholy and despair marked upon their countenances. Here again another scene of grief and lamentation arises;—friends and near relations must be parted never to meet again, nor knowing to whence they go. Here daughters are clinging to their mothers, and mothers to their daughters, bedewing each others naked breasts with tears; here fathers, mothers, and children, locked in each others arms, are begging never to be separated; here the husband will be pleading for his wife, and the wife praying for her children, and entreating, enough to melt the most obdurate heart, not to be torn from them, and taken away from her husband; and some will be still weeping for their native shore, and their dear relations and friends, and other endearing connections which they have left behind, and have been barbarously tore away from; and all are bemoaning themselves with grief and lamentation at the prospect of their wretched fate. And when sold and delivered up to their inhuman purchasers, a more heart-piercing scene cannot well take place. The last embrace of the beloved husband and wife may be seen, taking their dear offspring in their arms, and with the most parental fondness, bathing their cheeks with a final parting endearment. But on this occasion they are not permitted to continue long, they are soon torn away by their unfeeling masters, entirely destitute of a hope of ever seeing each other again; and no consolation is afforded to them in this sorrowful and truly pitiable situation. Should any of them still linger, and cling together a little longer, and not part as readily as their owners would have them, the flogger is called on, and they are soon drove away with the bloody commiseration of the cutting fangs of the whip lashing their naked bodies. This last exercise of the bloody whip, with many other cruel punishments, generally becomes an appendage of their miserable fate, until their wretched lives be wore out with hunger, nakedness, hard labour, dejection and despair. Alas! alas! poor unhappy mortal! to experience such treatment from men that take upon themselves the sacred name of Christians!

In such a vast extended, hideous and predominant slavery, as the Europeans carry on in their Colonies, some indeed may fall into better hands, and meet with some commiseration and better treatment than others, and a few may become free, and get themselves liberated from that cruel and galling yoke of bondage; but what are these to the whole, even hundreds of thousands, held and perpetrated in all the prevalent and intolerable calamities of that state of bondage and exile. The emancipation of a few, while ever that evil and predominant business of slavery is continued, cannot make that horrible traffic one bit the less criminal. For, according to the methods of procuring slaves in Africa, there must be great robberies and murders committed before any emancipation can take place, and before any lenitive favours can be shewn to any of them, even by the generous and humane. This must evidence that the whole of that base traffic is an enormous evil and wicked thing, which cries aloud for redress, and that an immediate end and stop should be put to it.

The worthy and judicious author of the Historical account of Guinea, and others, have given some very striking estimates of the exceeding evil occasioned by that wicked diabolical traffic of the African slave-trade; wherein it seems, of late years, the English have taken the lead, or the greatest part of it, in carrying it on. They have computed, that the ships from Liverpool, Bristol and London have exported from the coast of Africa upwards of one hundred thousand slaves annually; and that among other evils attending this barbarous inhuman traffic, it is also computed that the numbers which are killed by the treacherous and barbarous methods of procuring them, together with those that perish in the voyage, and die in the seasoning, amount to at least an hundred thousand, which perish in every yearly attempt to supply the colonies, before any of the wretched survivers, reduced to about sixty thousand, annually required as an additional stock can be made useful. But as the great severities and oppressions loaded upon the wretched survivors are such that they are continually wearing out, and a new annual supply wanted; that the vast carnage, and the great multitude of human souls that are actually deprived of life by carrying on that iniquitous business, may be supposed to be even more than one hundred thousand that perish annually; or supposing that to be greatly less than it is, still it is so great that the very idea is shocking to conceive, at the thought of it sensibility would blush, and feeling nature absolutely turn pale.

"Gracious God! how wicked, how beyond all example impious, must be that servitude which cannot be carried on without the continual murder of so many innocent persons. What punishment is not to be expected from such monstrous and unparalleled barbarity? For if the blood of one man unjustly shed cries with so loud a voice for the Divine vengeance, how shall the cries and groans of an hundred thousand men annually murdered ascend the celestial mansions, and bring down that punishment such enormities deserve?" As this enormous iniquity is not conjecture, but an obvious fact, occasioned by that dreadful and wicked business of slavery, were the inhabitants of Great-Britain to hear tell of any other nation that murdered one hundred thousand innocent people annually, they would think them an exceeding inhuman, barbarous, and wicked people indeed, and that they would be surely punished by some signal judgment of Almighty God. But surely law and liberty, justice and equity, which are the proper foundations of the British government, and humanity the most amiable characteristic of the people, must be entirely fled from their land, if they can think a less punishment due to themselves, for supporting and carrying on such enormous wickedness, if they do not speedily relinquish and give it up. The very nature of that wickedness of enslaving of men is such, that were the traffic, which European nations carry on in it, a thousand times less than it is, it would be what no righteous nation would admit of for the sake of any gain whatsoever. Wherefore as it is, what ought to be done? If there is any righteousness, any wisdom, any justice, or any humanity to be found, ought not the whole of it, and all the branches of such exceeding evil and wicked traffic, and all the iniquity of it to be relinquished, and root and branches to be speedily given up and put an end to?

"For while such monstrous iniquity, such deliberate barbarity and cruelty is carried on, whether it be considered as the crime of individuals, or as patronized and encouraged by the laws of the land, it holds forth an equal degree of enormity. And a crime founded in such a dreadful pre-eminence in wickedness, both of individuals and the nation, must some time draw down upon them the heaviest judgments of Almighty God." — "On this occasion there seems already to be an interference of Divine Providence, though the obdurate and impenitent part of mankind may not regard it. The violent and supernatural agitations of all the elements, which for a series of years have prevailed in those European settlements where the unfortunate Africans are retained in a state of slavery, and which have brought unspeakable calamities to the inhabitants, and public losses to the states to which they severally belong, are so many awful visitations of God for this inhuman violation of his laws. And it is not perhaps unworthy of remark, that as the subjects of Great-Britain have two-thirds of this impious commerce in their own hands, so they have suffered in the same proportioh, or more severely than the rest. How far these misfortunes may appear to be acts of Providence, and to create an alarm to those who have been accustomed to refer every effect to its apparent cause; who have been habituated to stop there, and to overlook the finger of God, because it is slightly covered under the veil of secondary laws, we will not pretend to determine; but this we will assert with confidence, that the Europeans have richly deserved them all: the fear of sympathy that can hardly be restrained on other melancholy occasions, seems to forget to flow at the relation of these; and that we can never, with any shadow of justice, wish prosperity to the undertakers of those whose success must be at the expence of the happiness of millions of their fellow-creatures*."

For though this world is not the place of final retribution, yet there is an evidence maintained in the course of Divine Providence, that verily there is a God that judgeth in the earth. That nations may continue long, with a considerable degree of worldly prosperity, and without seeming to be distinguished by remarkable calamities. when their wickedness is become very great and prevalent; yet it is no way inconsistent to assert, (and what sacred history warrant us to conclude) that their judgment slumbereth not. Had one been among the Canaanites a few years before the Israelites entered their country, or in Babylon a little before Cyrus encamped against it, he would have beheld a people in a state of great worldly prosperity, and in much security, notwithstanding that the judgments of God were ready to seize upon them. Great and destructive wars are kindled up from time to time, whereby multitudes of mankind are swept away from the face of the earth, and the wealth of nations are exhausted. Famine, pestilence and earthquakes have often spread terror, desolation and misery among the inhabitants of the world. Nor are there wanting instances of remarkable national distresses as a judgment for their wickedness, by a variety of other causes. Though men cannot easily be prevailed with to regard these as the operation of the hand of God, the scriptures, which contain the rules and history of Divine Providence, represent these as inflicted for the sins of nations, and not merely as casual things, for which no account can be given. And therefore some of these causes which may seem natural, and which have begun to make their appearance, and the annual destructions thereof, which are constantly heard of in some part or other, may be considered as tokens of God's judgments against the British empire, and a variety of them might be named; such as loss of territory and destructive wars, earthquakes and dreadful thunders, storms and hurricanes, blastings and destructive insects, inclement and

---

* See the excellent Mr. Clarkson's Essay on the Slavery and Commerce of the Human Species; and, I must add, the amiable and indefatigable friend of mankind, Granville Sharp, Esq; from whose writings I have borrowed some of the following observations. I am also indebted to several others, whose intrinsic virtues will equally shine in the same amiable manner, while ever there is any virtue and humanity amongst men; and when those of the enslavers of men will sink into abhorrence for ever.

unfruitful seasons, national debt and oppressions, poverty and distresses of individuals, &c. *For his own iniquity shall take the wicked himself,* and who can tell what dreadful calamities may yet befal to a people responsible for so great a share of iniquity as in that part which they carry on of the African slave-trade alone. "And it is not known how soon a just national retribution of vengeance may burst forth against it; how soon the Almighty may think fit to recompence the British nation, according to the work, of their hands, for the horrible oppression of the poor Africans."

"For national wickedness from the beginning of the world has generally been visited with national punishments; and surely no national wickedness can be more heinous in the sight of God than a public toleration of slavery, and sooner or later these kingdom will be visited with some signal mark of his displeasure, for the notorious oppression of the poor Africans, that are harassed and continually wearing out with a most shameful involuntary servitude in the British colonies, and by a public toleration under the sanction of laws, to which the monarchs of England from time to time, by advice of their privy counsellors, have given the royal assent, and thereby rendered themselves parties in the oppression, and it may be feared partakers in their guilt." — "And every man has ample reason to fear that God will make of this nation, in proportion to the magnitude of its guilt in the slave-dealing, a tremendous example of retribution to deter other nations from offending his eternal justice, if a sincere and speedy repentance does not avert it." — "For such notorious crimes the Almighty, even the Lord, hath sworn, *surely I will never forget any of these works.*" See Amos viii. But the judgments of God are often suspended and mitigated for the sake of the righteous; and nations are preserved from destruction in favour to them who remain faithful in times of general defection. Isaiah i. 9. "Except the Lord of Hosts had left us a very small remnant, we should have been as Sodom, and we should have been like unto Gomorah."

But while ever such a horrible business as the slavery and oppression of the Africans is carried on, there is not one man in all Great-Britain and her colonies, that knoweth any thing of it, can be innocent and safe, unless he speedily riseth up with abhorrence of it in his own judgment, and, to avert evil, declare himself against it, and all such notorious wickedness. But should the contrary be adhered to, as it has been in the most shameful manner, by men of eminence and power; according to their eminence in station, the nobles and senators, and every man in office and authority, must incur a double load of guilt, and not only that burden of guilt in the oppression of the African strangers, but also in that of an impending danger and ruin to their country; and such a double load of iniquity must rest upon those guilty heads who withhold their testimony against the crying sin of tolerating slavery. The inhabitants in general who can approve of such inhuman barbarities, must themselves be a species of unjust barbarians and inhuman men. But the clergy of all denominations, whom we would consider as the devout messengers of righteousness, peace, and good-will to all men, if we find any of them ranked with infidels and barbarians, we must consider them as particularly responsible, and, in some measure, guilty of the crimes of other wicked men in the highest degree. For it is their duty to warn every man, and to teach every man to know their errors; and if they do not, the crimes of those under their particular charge must rest upon themselves, and upon some of them, in such a case as this, that of the whole nation in general; and those (whatever their respective situation may be) who forbid others to assist them, must not be very sensible of their own duty, and the great extensiveness and importance of their own charge. And as it is their great duty to teach men righteousness and piety; this ought to be considered as sufficiently obvious unto them, and to all men, that nothing can be more contrary unto it, than the evil and very nature of enslaving men, and making merchandize of them like the brute creation. "For it is evident that no custom established among men was ever more impious; since it is contrary to reason, justice, nature, the principles of law and government, and the whole doctrine, in short, of natural religion, and the revealed voice of God. And, therefore, that it is both evident and expedient, that there is an absolute necessity to abolish the slave trade, and the West-India slavery; and that to be in power, and to neglect even a day in endeavouring to put a stop to such monstrous iniquity and abandoned wickedness (as the tenure of every man's life, as well as the time of his being in office and power is very uncertain) must necessarily endanger a man's own eternal welfare, be he ever so great in temporal dignity."

The higher that any man is exalted in power and dignity, his danger is the more eminent, though he may not live to see the evil that may eventually be contributed to his country, because of his disobedience to the law and commandments of God. All men in authority, and kings in general, who are exalted to the most conspicuous offices of superiority, while they take upon themselves to be the administrators of righteousness and justice to others, they become equally responsible for admitting or suffering others under their authority to do wrong. Wherefore the highest offices of authority among men, are not so desirable as some may be apt to conceive; it was so considered by the virtuous queen Anne, when she was called to the royal dignity, as she declared to the council of the nation, that it was a heavy weight and burden brought upon her. For kings are the ministers of God, to do justice, and not to bear the sword in vain, but to revenge wrath upon them that do evil. But if they do not in such a case as this, the cruel oppressions of thousands, and the blood of the murdered Africans who are slain by the sword of cruel avarice, must rest upon their own guilty heads in as eventually and plain a sense as it was David that murdered Uriah; and therefore they ought to let no companies of insidious merchants, or any guileful insinuations of wicked men, prevail upon them to establish laws of iniquity, and to carry on a trade of oppression and injustice; but they ought to consider such as the worst of foes and rebels, and greater enemies than any that can rise up against their temporal dignity. From all such enemies, good Lord, deliver them! for it is even better to lose a temporal kingdom, than only to endanger the happiness and enjoyment of an eternal one.

Nothing else can be conceived, but that the power of infernal wickedness has so reigned and pervaded over the enlightened nations, as to infatuate and lead on the great men, and the kings of Europe, to promote and establish such a horrible traffic of wickedness as the African slave trade and the West-India slavery, and thereby to bring themselves under the guilty responsibility of such awful iniquity. The kings and governors of the nations in general have power to prevent their subjects and people from enslaving and oppressing others, if they will; but if they do not endeavour to do it, even if they could not effect that good purpose, they must then be responsible for their crimes; how much more, if they make no endeavours towards it, even when they can, and where no opposition, however plausible their pretences might be, would dare to oppose them. Wherefore, if kings or nations, or any men that dealeth unjustly with their fellow-creatures, to ensnare them, to enslave them, and to oppress them, or suffer others to do so, when they have it in their power to prevent it, and yet they do not, can it ever be thought that God will be well pleased with them? For can those which have no mercy on their fellow-creatures, expect to find mercy from the gracious Father of Men? Or will it not rather be said unto them, as it is declared, *that he who leadeth into captivity, shall be carried captive, and be bound in the cords of his own iniquity: Though hand join in hand the wicked shall not go unpunished; for sin and wickedness is the destruction of any people.* And should these nations, in the most obnoxious and tenacious manner, still adhere to it as they have done, and continue to carry on in their colonies such works and purposes of iniquity, in oppression and injustice against the Africans, nothing else can be expected for them at last, but to meet with the fierce wrath of Almighty God, for such a combination of wickedness, according to all the examples of his just retribution, who cannot suffer such deliberate, such monstrous iniquity to go long unpunished.

There is good reason to suppose, that it was far from the intention of Ferdinand, king of Spain, to use his new subjects in America in the brutal and barbarous manner that his people did; and happy for the credit of that nation, and the honor of mankind, even among the profligate adventurers which were sent to conquer and desolate the new world, there were some persons that retained some tincture of virtue and generosity, and some men of the greatest reputation of both gentlemen and clergy, which did not only remonstrate, but protest against their measures then carried on. And since that iniquitous traffic of slavery has commenced and been carried on, many gentlemen of the most distinguished reputation, of different nations, and particularly in England, have protested and remonstrated against it. But the guileful insinuations of avaricious wicked men, which prevailed formerly, have still been continued; and to answer the purposes of their own covetousness, the different nations have been fomented with jealousy to one another, least another should have the advantage in any traffic; and while naturally emulous to promote their own ambition, they have imbrewed their hands in that infamous commerce of iniquity; and by the insidious instigation of those whose private emolument depends on it, the various profligate adventurers, from time to time, have acquired the sanction of laws to support them, and have obtained the patronage of kings in their favour to encourage them, whereby that commerce of the most notorious injustice, and open violation of the laws of God, hath been carried on exceedingly to the shame of all the Christian nations, and greatly to the disgrace of all the monarchs of Europe. The fact speaks itself: *And destruction shall be to the workers of iniquity.* The bold and oftensive enslavers of men, who subject their fellow-creatures to the rank of a brute, and the immolate value of a beast, are themselves the most abandoned slaves of infernal wickedness, the most obnoxious ruffians among men, the enemies of their country, and the disgrace of kings. Their iniquity is wrote in the light as with a sun-beam, and engraven on the hardest rock as with the point of a diamond, that cannot be easily wiped away: *But the wicked shall fall by their own wickedness.* And, nevertheless, by the insidious instigations of those who have forsaken the amiable virtues of men, and have acquired the cruel ferocity of tygers and wild beasts, they have not only polluted themselves with their iniquity, but their base treachery has brought shame and guilt upon some of the most exalted and most amiable characters in the world. And, therefore, that no evil may happen unto those who have been so shamefully beguiled and betrayed by the vile instigations of wicked, profligate, inhuman men, and that no shame and guilt may rest upon him, who standeth in the greatest eminence of responsibility, I would ever desire to pray; let all the prayers of the wise and pious be heard for the king, and for his wise counsellors, and the great men that stand before him; for kings and great men stand in the most perilous situation of having the crimes of others imputed to them; wherefore kings have need of all your prayers, that the counsel of the wicked may not prevail against them, for these are the worst foes, and most terrible enemies, both to yourselves and to your sovereign. *Righteousness exalteth a nation, but sin is a reproach to any people.*

In this advanced æra, when the kings of Europe are become more conspicuous for their manly virtues, than any before them have been, it is to be hoped that they will not any longer suffer themselves to be imposed upon, and be beguiled, and brought into guilt and shame, by any instigations of the cunning craftiness and evil policy of the avaricious, and the vile profligate enslavers of men. And as their wisdom and understanding is great, and exalted as their high dignity, it is also to be hoped that they will exert themselves, in the cause of righteousness and justice, and be like the wisest and the greatest monarchs of old, to hearken to the counsel of the wise men that know the times, and to the righteous laws of God, and to deliver the oppressed, and to put an end to the iniquitous commerce and slavery of men. And as we hear tell of the kings of Europe having almost abolished, the infernal invention of the bloody tribunal of the inquisition, and the Emperor and others making some grand reformations for the happiness and good of their subjects; it is to be hoped also that these exalted and liberal principles

will lead them on to greater improvements in civilization and felicitation, and next to abolish that other diabolical invention of the bloody
and cruel African slave-trade, and the West-Indian slavery.

But whereas the people of Great-Britain having now acquired a
greater share in that iniquitous commerce than all the rest together,
they are the first that ought to set an example, lest they have to repent
for their wickedness when it becomes too late; lest some impending calamity should speedily burst forth against them, and lest a just retribution for their enormous crimes, and a continuance in committing similar deeds of barbarity and injustice should involve them in ruin. For we
may be assured that God will certainly avenge himself of such heinous
transgressors of his law, and of all those planters and merchants, and
of all others, who are the authors of the Africans graves, severities, and
cruel punishments, and no plea of any absolute necessity can possibly
excuse them. And as the inhabitants of Great-Britain, and the inhabitants of the colonies, seem almost equally guilty of the oppression,
there is great reason for both to dread the severe vengeance of Almighty
God upon them, and upon all such notorious workers of wickedness;
for it is evident that the legislature of Great-Britain patronises and en-
courages them, and shares in the infamous profits of the slavery of the
Africans. It is therefore necessary that the inhabitants of the British
nation should seriously consider these things for their own good and
safety, as well as for our benefit and deliverance, and that they may be
sensible of their own error and danger, lest they provoke the vengeance
of the Almighty against them. For what wickedness was there ever risen
up so monstrous, and more likely to bring a heavy rod of destruction
upon a nation, than the deeds committed by the West-Indian slavery,
and the African slave trade. And even in that part of it carried on by
the Liverpool and Bristol merchants, the many shocking and inhuman
instances of their barbarity and cruelty are such, that every one that
heareth thereof has reason to tremble, and cry out, *Should not the land
tremble for this, and every one mourn that dwelleth therein?*

The vast carnage and murders committed by the British instigators of slavery, is attended with a very shocking, peculiar, and almost
unheard of conception, according to the notion of the perpetrators of
it; they either consider them as their own property, that they may do
with as they please, in life or death; or that the taking away the life of
a black man is of no more account than taking away the life of a beast.
A very melancholy instance of this happened about the year 1780, as

recorded in the courts of law; a master of a vessel bound to the Western Colonies, selected 132 of the most sickly of the black slaves, and ordered them to be thrown overboard into the sea, in order to recover their value from the insurers, as he had perceived that he was too late to get a good market for them in the West-Indies. On the trial, by the counsel for the owners of the vessel against the underwriters, their argument was, that the slaves were to be considered the same as horses; and their plea for throwing them into the sea, was nothing better than that it might be more necessary to throw them overboard to lighten their vessel than goods of greater value, or something to that effect. These poor creatures, it seems, were tied two and two together when they were thrown into the sea, lest some of them might swim a little for the last gasp of air, and, with the animation of their approaching exit, breath their souls away to the gracious Father of spirits. Some of the last parcel, when they saw the fate of their companions, made their escape from tying by jumping overboard, and one was saved by means of a rope from some in the ship. The owners of the vessel, I suppose, (inhuman connivers of robbery, slavery, murder and fraud) were rather a little defeated in this, by bringing their villainy to light in a court of law; but the inhuman monster of a captain was kept out of the way of justice from getting hold of him. Though such perpetrators of murder and fraud should have been sought after from the British Dan in the East-Indies, to her Beershebah in the West.

But our lives are accounted of no value, we are hunted after as the prey in the desart, and doomed to destruction as the beasts that perish. And for this, should we appeal to the inhabitants of Europe, would they dare to say that they have not wronged us, and grievously injured us, and that the blood of millions do not cry out against them? And if we appeal to the inhabitants of Great-Britain, can they justify the deeds of their conduct towards us? And is it not strange to think, that they who ought to be considered as the most learned and civilized people in the world, that they should carry on a traffic of the most barbarous cruelty and injustice, and that many, even among them, are become so dissolute, as to think slavery, robbery and murder no crimes? But we will answer to this, that no man can, with impunity, steal, kidnap, buy or sell another man, without being guilty of the most atrocious villainy. And we will aver, that every slave-holder that claims any property in slaves, or holds them in an involuntary servitude, are the most obnoxious and dissolute robbers among men; and that they have no more right, nor any better title to any one of them, than the most profligate and notorious robbers and thieves in the world, has to the goods which they have robbed and stole from the right owners and lawful possessor thereof. But should the slave-holders say that they buy them; their title and claim is no better then that of the most notorious conniver, who buys goods from other robbers, knowing them to be stole and accordingly gives an inferior price for them. According to the laws of England, when such connivers are discovered, and the property of others unlawfully found in their possession; the right owners thereof can oblige the connivers to restore back their property, and to punish them for their trespass. But the slave-holders, universally, are those connivers, they do not only rob men of some of their property, but they keep men from every property belonging to them, and compel them to their involuntary service and drudgery; and those whom they buy from other robbers, and keep in their possession, are greatly injured by them when compared to any species of goods whatsoever; and accordingly they give but a very inferior price for men, as all their vast estates in the West-Indies is not sufficient to buy one of them, if the rightful possessor was to sell himself to them in the manner that they claim possession of him. Therefore let the inhabitants of any civilized nation determine, whether, if they were to be treated in the same manner that the Africans are, by various pirates, kidnappers, and slave-holders, and their wives, and their sons and daughters were to be robbed from them, or themselves violently taken away to a perpetual and intolerable slavery; or whether they would not think those robbers, who only took away their property, less injurious to them than the other. If they determine it so, as reason must tell every man, that himself is of more value than his property; then the executors of the laws of civilization ought to tremble at the inconsistency of passing judgment upon those whose crimes, in many cases, are less than what the whole legislature must be guilty of, when those of a far greater is encouraged and supported by it wherever slavery is tolerated by law, and, consequently, that slavery can no where be tolerated with any consistency to civilization and the laws of justice among men; but if it can maintain its ground, to have any place at all, it must be among a society of barbarians and thieves, and where the laws of their society is, for every one to catch what he can. Then, when theft and robbery becomes no crimes, the man-stealer and the conniving slave-holder might possibly get free.

But the several nations of Europe that have joined in that iniquitous traffic of buying, selling and enslaving men, must in course have left their own laws of civilization to adopt those of barbarians and robbers, and that they may say to one another, *When thou sawest a thief, then thou consentest with him, and hast been partaker with all the workers of iniquity.* But whereas every man, as a rational creature, is responsible for his actions, and he becomes not only guilty in doing evil himself, but in letting others rob and oppress their fellow-creatures with impunity, or in not delivering the oppressed when he has it in his power to help them. And likewise that nation which may be supposed to maintain a very considerable degree of civilization, justice and equity within its own jurisdiction, is not in that case innocent, while it beholds another nation or people carrying on persecution, oppression and slavery, unless it remonstrates against that wickedness of the other nation, and makes use of every effort in its power to help the oppressed, and to rescue the innocent. For so it ought to be the universal rule of duty to all men that fear God and keep his commandments, to do good to all men wherever they can; and when they find any wronged and injured by others, they should endeavour to deliver the ensnared whatever their grievances may be; and should this sometimes lead them into war they might expect the protection and blessing of heaven. How far other motives may appear eligible for men to oppose one another with hostile force, it is not my business to enquire. But I should suppose the hardy veterans who engage merely about the purposes of envying one another concerning any different advantages of commerce, or for enlarging their territories and dominions, or for the end of getting riches by their conquest; that if they fall in the combat, they must generally die, as the fool dieth, vaunting in vain glory; and many of them be like to those who go out in darkness, never to see light; and should they come off alive, what more does their honour and same amount to, but only to be like that antediluvian conqueror, *who had slain a man to his own wounding, and a young man to his hurt.* But those mighty men of renown in the days of old, because of their apostacy from God, and rebellion and wickedness to men, were at last all swallowed up by an universal deluge for their iniquity and crimes.

But again let me observe, that whatever civilization the inhabitants of Great-Britain may enjoy among themselves, they have seldom maintained their own innocence in that great duty as a Christian nation towards others; and I may say, with respect to their African neighbours, or to any other wheresover they may go by the way of commerce, they have not regarded them at all. And when they saw others robbing the Africans, and carrying them into captivity and slavery, they have neither helped them, nor opposed their oppressors in the least. But instead thereof they have joined in combination against them with the rest of other profligate nations and people, to buy, enslave and make merchandize of them, because they found them helpless and fit to suit their own purpose, and are become the head carriers on of that iniquitous traffic. But the greater that any reformation and civilization is obtained by any nation, if they do not maintain righteousness, but carry on any course of wickedness and oppression, it makes them appear only the more inconsistent, and their tyranny and oppression the more conspicuous. Wherefore because of the great wickedness, cruelty and injustice done to the Africans, those who are greatest in the transgression give an evident and undubious warrant to all other nations beholding their tyranny and injustice to others, if those nations have any regard to their own innocence and virtue, and wish to maintain righteousness, and to remain clear of the oppression and blood of all men; it is their duty to chastize and suppress such unjust and tyrannical oppressors and enslavers of men. And should none of these be found among the enlightened and civilized nations, who maintain their own innocence and righteousness, with regard to their duty unto all men; and that there may be none to chastize the tyrannical oppressors of others; then it may be feared, as it has often been, that fierce nations of various insects, and other annoyances, may be sent as a judgment to punish the wicked nations of men. For by some way or other every criminal nation, and all their confederates, who sin and rebel against God, and against his laws of nature and nations, will each meet with some awful retribution at last, unless they repent of their iniquity. And the greater advantages of light, learning, knowledge and civilization that any people enjoy, if they do not maintain righteousness, but do wickedly, they will meet with the more severe rebuke when the visitations of God's judgment cometh upon them. And the prophecy which was given to Moses, is still as much in force against the enlightened nations now for their wickedness, in going after the abominations of heathens and barbarians, for none else would attempt to enslave and make merchandize of men, as it was when denounced against the Israelitish nation of old, when they departed, or should depart, from the laws and statutes of the Most High. *The Lord shall bring a nation against thee, from far, from the ends of the earth, as swift as the eagle flieth, a nation whose tongue thou shalt not understand,* &c. See Deut. xxviii.

But lest any of these things should happen to the generous and respectful Britons, who are not altogether lost to virtue and consideration; let me say unto you, in the language of a wise and eminent Queen, as she did when her people were sold as a prey to their enemies: That it is not all your enemies (for they can be reckoned nothing else), the covetous instigators and carriers on of slavery and wickedness, that can in any way countervail the damage to yourselves, to your king, and to your country; nor will all the infamous profits of the poor Africans avail you any thing if it brings down the avenging hand of God upon you. We are not saying that we have not sinned, and that we are not deserving of the righteous judgments of God against us. But the enemies that have risen up against us are cruel, oppressive and unjust; and their haughtiness of insolence, wickedness and iniquity is like to that of Haman the son of Hammedatha; and who dare suppose, or even presume to think, that the inhuman ruffians and ensnarers of men, the vile negociators and merchandizers of the human species, and the offensive combinations of slave-holders in the West have done no evil? And should we be passive, as the suffering martyrs dying in the flames, whose blood crieth for vengeance on their persecutors and murderers; so the iniquity of our oppressors, enslavers and murderers rise up against them. For we have been hunted after as the wild beasts of the earth, and sold to the enemies of mankind as their prey; and should any of us have endeavoured to get away from them, as a man would naturally fly from an enemy that way-laid him; we have been pursued after, and, by haughty mandates and laws of iniquity, overtaken, and murdered and slain, and the blood of millions cries out against them. And together with these that have been cruelly spoiled and slain, the very grievous afflictions that we have long suffered under, has been long crying for vengeance on our oppressors; and the great distress and wretchedness of human woe and misery, which we are yet lying under, is still rising up before that High and Sovereign Hand of Justice, where men, by all their oppression and cruelty, can no way prevent; their evil treatment of others may serve to increase the blow, but not to evade the stroke of His power, nor withhold the bringing down that arm of vengeance on themselves, and upon all their connivers and confederators, and the particular instigators of such wilful murders and inhuman barbarity. The life of a black man is of as much regard in the sight of

God, as the life of any other man; though we have been sold as a carnage to the market, and as a prey to profligate wicked men, to torture
and lash us as they please, and as their caprice may think fit, to murder
us at discretion.

And should any of the best of them plead, as they generally will
do, and tell of their humanity and charity to those whom they have
captured and enslaved, their tribute of thanks is but small; for what is
it, but a little restored to the wretched and miserable whom they have
robbed of their all; and only to be dealt with, like the spoils of those
taken in the field of battle, where the wretched fugitives must submit
to what they please. For as we have been robbed of our natural right as
men, and treated as beasts, those who have injured us, are like to them
who have robbed the widow, the orphans, the poor and the needy of
their right, and whose children are rioting on the spoils of those who
are begging at their doors for bread. And should they say, that their
fathers were thieves and connivers with ensnarers of men, and that
they have been brought up to the iniquitous practice of slavery and oppression of their fellow-creatures and they cannot live without carrying
it on, and making their gain by the unlawful merchandize and cruel
slavery of men, what is that to us, and where will it justify them? And
some will be saying, that the Black people, who are free in the West Indies, are more miserable than the slaves;—and well they may; for while
they can get their work and drudgery done for nothing, it is not likely
that they will employ those whom they must pay for their labour. But
whatever necessity the enslavers of men may plead for their iniquitous
practice of slavery, and the various advantages which they get by it, can
only evidence their own injustice and dishonesty. A man that is truly
honest, fears nothing so much as the very imputation of injustice; but
those men who dare not face the consequence of acting uprightly in
every case are detestable cowards, unworthy the name of men; for it is
manifest that such men are more afraid of temporal inconveniencies
than they are of God: *And I say unto you, my friends, be not afraid of
them that kill the body, and after that have no more that they can do; but I
will forwarn you whom you shall fear: Fear him, who, after he hath killed,
hath power to cast into hell.* Luke xii.4, 5.

But why should a total abolition, and an universal emancipation
of slaves, and the enfranchisement of all the Black People employed in
the culture of the Colonies, taking place as it ought to do, and without
any hesitation, or delay for a moment, even though it might have some

seeming appearance of loss either to government or to individuals, be feared at all? Their labour, as freemen, would be as useful in the sugar colonies as any other class of men that could be found; and should it even take place in such a manner that some individuals, at first, would suffer loss as a just reward for their wickedness in slave-dealing, what is that to the happiness and good of doing justice to others; and, I must say, to the great danger, otherwise, that must eventually hang over the whole community? It is certain, that the produce of the labour of slaves, together with all the advantages of the West-India traffic, bring in an immense revenue to government; but let that amount be what it will, there might be as much or more expected from the labour of an equal increase of free people, and without the implication of any guilt attending it, and which, otherwise, must be a greater burden to bear, and more ruinous consequences to be feared from it, than if the whole national debt was to sink at once, and to rest upon the heads of all that might suffer by it. Whereas, if a generous encouragement were to be given to a free people, peaceable among themselves, intelligent and industrious, who by art and labour would improve the most barren situations, and make the most of that which is fruitful; the free and voluntary labour of many, would soon yield to any government, many greater advantages than any thing that slavery can produce. And this should be expected, wherever a Christian government is extended, and the true religion is embraced, that the blessings of liberty should be extended likewise, and that it should diffuse its influences first to fertilize the mind, and then the effects of its benignity would extend, and arise with exuberant blessings and advantages from all its operations. Was this to be the case, every thing would increase and prosper at home and abroad, and ten thousand times greater and greater advantages would arise to the state, and more permanent and solid benefit to individuals from the service of freemen, than ever they can reap, or in any possible way enjoy, by the labour of slaves.

But why this diabolical traffic of slavery has not been abolished before now, and why it was introduced at all, as I have already enquired, must be greatly imputed to that powerful and pervading agency of infernal wickedness, which reigneth and prevaileth over the nations, and to that umbrageous image of iniquity established thereby; for had there been any truth and righteousness in that grand horn of delusion in the east, which may seem admirable to some, and be looked upon by its votaries as the fine burnished gold, and bright as the finest polished silver, then would not slavery, cruelty and oppression have been abolished wherever its influence came? And had the grand apostacy of its fellow horn, with all its lineaments been any better, and endowed with any real virtue and goodness, whom its devotees may behold as the finest polished diamond, and glistening as the finest gems, then would not slavery and barbarity have been prohibited and forbidden wherever the beams of any Christianity arose? Then might we have expected to hear tidings of good, even from thou who are gone to repose in the fabulous paradise of Mahomet? Then might we have looked for it from those who are now reclined to slumber in assimulation with the old dotards of Rome, or to those who are fallen asleep and become enamoured with the scarlet couch of the abominable enchantress dyed in blood? And as well then might we not expect tenderness and compassion from those whom the goddess of avarice has so allured with her charms, that her heart-sick lovers are become reversed to the feelings of human woe; and with the great hurry and bustle of the russet slaves employed in all the drudgeries of the western isles, and maritime shore, in the cruel and involuntary service of her voluptuousness, having so dazzled their eyes, and bereaved them of all sensibility, that their hearts are become callous as the nether millstone, fierce as the tygers, and devoid of the natural feelings of men? From all such enchantments we would turn away, and fly from them as from the ravenous beasts of prey, as from the weeping crocodiles and the devouring reptiles, and as from the hoary monsters of the deep.

But we would look unto you, O ye multitude in the desert! against whom there is no enchantment, neither any divination whatever, that can prevail against you! for in your mouth there is no error or guile to be found, nor any fault before the throne of God. And what! though your dwellings be in all lands, and ye have no nation or kingdom on earth that ye can call your own, and your camp be surrounded with many enemies, yet you have a place of defence, an invincible fortress, the munitions of rocks for your refuge, and the shield of your anointed is Almighty; and behold his buckler is strong, and his sceptre is exalted on high, and the throne of his dominion and power ruleth over all. But in the day that we shall be spoken for, if we find you a wall, we would build upon you a palace of silver; and if you find us a door, inclose us with boards of cedar, for we long, and would to God that we longed more, to enter into your fortress, and follow you to your happy retreat. Then might we, like you, stand undaunted before our foes, and with more than heroic sullenness at all their cruel tortures, highly disdain their rage, and boldly dare them to do their worst. For you, O ye friends of the Most High, when you die, when ye are persecuted and slain, when you fall in the combat, when you die in the battle, it is you! only you, that come off conquerors, and more than conquerors through him that loved you! And should it yet be, as it has often been, that your foes might pursue you with their usual arrogance and persecuting rage, and cause you to die cruelly veiled in a curtain of blood, lo! your stains are all washed away, and your wounds and scars will soon be healed, and yourselves will be then invested with a robe of honor that will shine in whiteness for ever new, and your blood that was shed by the terrific rage of your foes, will testify against them, and rise up in grandeur to you, as an enfringement of gold floating in glory, and as his robe of honor which flames in eternal crimson through the heavens. But we envy no man, but wish them to do good, and not evil; and we want the prayers of the good, and whereever they can to help us; and the blessing of God be with all the promoters of righteousness and peace.

But wherefore, O beloved, should your watchmen sit still, when they hear tell that the enemy is invading all the out-posts and camp of the British empire, where many of your dwellings are? Are they all fallen asleep, and lying down to slumber in assimilation with the workers of iniquity? Should not those who are awake, arise, and give the alarm, that others may arise and awake also? And should not they who feareth the name of the Lord, and worship in his holy temples, *Let judgment to run down as waters, and righteousness as a mighty stream*? But why think ye prayers in churches and chapels only will do ye good, if your charity do not extend to pity and regard your fellow creatures perishing through ignorance, under the heavy yoke of subjection and bondage, to the cruel and avaricious oppression of brutish profligate men; and when both the injured, and their oppressors, dwell in such a vicinity as equally to claim your regard? The injurers, oppressors, enslavers, and murderers of others, eventually bring a curse upon themselves, as far as they destroy, injure, and cruelly and basely treat those under their subjection and unlawful bondage. And where such a dreadful pre-eminence of iniquity abounds, as the admission of laws for tolerating slavery and wickedness, and the worst of robberies, not only of men's proper|ties, but themselves; and the many inhuman murders and cruelties occasioned by it: If it meets with your approbation, it is your sin, and you are then as a conniver and confederator with those workers of wickedness; and if you give it a sanction by your passive obedience, it manifests that you are gone over to those brutish enemies of mankind, and can in no way be a true lover of your king and country.

Wherefore it ought to be the universal endeavour, and the ardent wish, of all the lovers of God and the Saviour of men, and of all that delight in his ways of righteousness, and of all the lovers of their country, and the friends of mankind, and of every real patriot in the land, and of every man and woman that dwelleth therein, and of all those that have any pretence to charity, generosity, sensibility and humanity, and whoever has any regard to innocence and virtue, to plead that slavery, with all its great and heinous magnitude of iniquity, might be abolished throughout all the British dominions; and from henceforth to hinder and prohibit the carrying on of that barbarous, brutish and inhuman traffic of the slavery and commerce of the human species, wherever the power and influence of the British empire extends. And in doing this, and always in doing righteously, let the glory and honour of it be alone ascribed unto God Most High, for his great mercy and goodness to you; and that his blessings and unbounded beneficence may shine forth upon you, and upon all the promoters of it: and that it may with great honours and advantages of peace and prosperity be ever resting upon the noble Britons, and upon their most worthy, most eminent and august Sovereign, and upon all his government and the people under it; and that the streams thereof may run down in righteousness even to us, poor deplorable Africans.

And we that are particularly concerned would humbly join with all the rest of our brethren and countrymen in complexion, who have been grievously injured, and who jointly and separately, in all the language of grief and woe, are humbly imploring and earnestly entreating the most respectful and generous people of Great-Britain, that they would consider us, and have mercy and compassion on us, and to take away that evil that your enemies, as well as our oppressors, are doing towards us, and cause them to desist from their evil treatment of the poor and despised Africans, before it be too late; and to restore that justice and liberty which is our natural right, that we have been unlawfully deprived and cruelly wronged of, and to deliver us from that captivity and bondage which we now suffer under, in our present languishing state of exile and misery. And we humbly pray that God may put it into the minds of the noble Britons, that they may have the honor and advantage of doing so great good to many, and to extend their power and influence to do good afar; and that great good in abundance may come down upon themselves, and upon all their government and the people under it, in every place belonging to the British empire. But if the people and the legislature of Great-Britain altogether hold their peace at such a time as this, and even laugh at our calamity as heretofore they have been wont to do, by making merchandize of us to enrich themselves with our misery and distress: we sit like the mourning Mordecai's at their gates cloathed in sackcloth; and, in this advanced era, we hope God in his Providence will rise up a deliverance for us some other way; and we have great reason to hope that the time of our deliverance is fast drawing nigh, and when the great Babylon of iniquity will fall.

And whereas we consider our case before God of the whole universe, the Gracious Father and Saviour of men; we will look unto him for help and deliverance. The cry of our affliction is already gone up before him, and he will hearken to the voice of our distress; for he hears the cries and groans of the oppressed, and professes that if they cry at all unto him, he will hearken unto them, and deliver them. *For the oppression of the poor, for the sighing of the needy, now will I arise saith Jehovah, and will set him in safety from him that puffeth at him or that would ensnare him.* (Psa. xii.5.) *And I know that Jehovah will maintain the cause of the afflicted, and the right of the poor.* (Psa. cxl.12.) Wherefore it is our duty to look up to a greater deliverer than that of the British nation, or of any nation upon earth; for unless God gives them repentance, and peace towards him, we can expect no peace or deliverance from them. But still we shall have cause to trust, that God who made of one blood all the nations and children of men, and who gave to all equally a natural right to liberty; that he who ruleth over all the kingdoms of the earth with equal providential justice, shall then make enlargement and deliverance to arise to the grievously injured, and heavy oppressed Africans from another place.

And as we look for our help and sure deliverance to come from God Most High, should it not come in an apparent way from Great-Britain, whom we consider as the Queen of nations, let her not think to escape more than others, if she continues to carry on oppression and injustice, and such pre-eminent wickedness against us: for we are only seeking that justice may be done to us, and what every righteous nation ought to do; and if it be not done, it will be adding iniquity to iniquity against themselves. But let us not suppose that the inhabitants of the British nation will adhere to the ways of the profligate: *For such is the way of an adulterous woman; she eateth, and wipeth her mouth; and saith, I have done no wickedness.* But rather let us suppose, *That whereas iniquity hath abounded, may righteousness much more abound.* For the wickedness that you have done is great, and wherever your traffic and colonies have been extended it is shameful; and the great injustice and cruelty done to the poor Africans crieth to heaven against you; and therefore that it may be forgiven unto you, it cries aloud for universal reformation and national repentance. But let it not suffice that a gracious call from the throne is inviting you, *To a religious observance of God's holy laws, as fearing, lest God's wrath and indignation, should be provoked against you*; but in your zeal for God's holy law, because of the shameful transgression thereof, every man every woman hath reason to mourn apart, and every one that dwelleth in the land ought to mourn and sigh for all the abominations done therein, and for the great wickedness carried on thereby.

And now that blessings may come instead of a curse, and that many beneficent purposes of good might speedily arise and flow from it, and be more readily promoted: I would hereby presume to offer the following considerations, as some outlines of a general reformation which ought to be established and carried on. And first, I would propose, that there ought to be days of mourning and fasting appointed, to make enquiry into that great and pre-eminent evil for many years past carried on against the Heathen nations, and the horrible iniquity of making merchandize of us, and cruelly enslaving the poor Africans: and that you might seek grace and repentance, and find mercy and forgiveness before God Omnipotent; and that he may give you wisdom and understanding to devise what ought to be done.

Secondly, I would propose that a total abolition of slavery should be made and proclaimed; and that an universal emancipation of slaves should begin from the date thereof, and be carried on in the following manner: That a proclamation should be caused to be made, setting forth the Antichristian unlawfulness of the slavery and commerce of the human species; and that it should be sent to all the courts and nations in Europe, to require their advice and assistance, and as they may find it unlawful to carry it on, let them whosoever will join to prohibit it. And if such a proclamation be found advisable to the British legislature, let them publish it, and cause it to be published, throughout all the British empire, to hinder and prohibit all men under their government to traffic either in buying or selling men; and to prevent it, a penalty might be made against it of one thousand pounds, for any man either to buy or sell another man. And that it should require all slave-holders, upon the immediate information thereof, to mitigate the labour of their slaves to that of a lawful servitude, without tortures or oppression; and that they should not hinder, but cause and procure some suitable means of instruction for them in the knowledge of the Christian religion. And agreeable to the late *royal Proclamation, for the Encouragement of Piety and Virtue, and for the preventing and punishing of Vice, Profaneness and Immorality*; that by no means, under any pretence whatsoever, either for themselves or their masters, the slaves under their subjection should not be suffered to work on the Sabbath days, unless it be such works as necessity and mercy may require. But that those days, as well as some other hours selected for the purpose, should be appropriated for the time of their instruction; and that if any of their owners should not provide such suitable instructors for them, that those slaves should be taken away from them and given to others who would maintain and instruct them for their labour. And that it should be made known to the slaves, that those who had been above seven years in the islands or elsewhere, if they had obtained any competent degree of knowledge of the Christian religion, and the laws of civilization, and had behaved themselves honestly and decently, that they should immediately become free; and that their owners should give them reasonable wages and maintenance for their labour, and not cause them to go away unless they could find some suitable employment elsewhere. And accordingly, from the date of their arrival to seven years, as they arrive at some suitable progress in knowledge, and behaved themselves honestly, that they should be getting free in the course of that time, and at the end of seven years to let every honest man and woman become free; for in the course of that time, they would have sufficiently paid their owners by their labour, both for their first purpose, and for the expences attending their education. By being thus instructed in the course of seven years, they would become tractable and obedient, useful labourers, dutiful servants and good subjects; and Christian men might have the honor and happiness to see many of them vieing with themselves to praise the God of their salvation. And it might be another necessary duty for Christians, in the course of that time, to make enquiry concerning some of their friends and relations in Africa: and if they found any intelligent persons amongst them, to give them as good education as they could, and find out a way of recourse to their friends; that as soon as they had made any progress in useful learning and the knowledge of the Christian religion, they might be sent back to Africa, to be made useful there as soon, and as many of them as could be made fit for instructing others. The rest would become useful residentors in the colonies; where there might be employment enough given to all free people, with suitable wages according to their usefulness, in the improvement of land; and the more encouragement that could be given to agriculture, and every other branch of useful industry, would thereby encrease the number of the inhabitants; without which any country, however blessed by nature, must continue poor.

And, thirdly, I would propose, that a fleet of some ships of war should be immediately sent to the coast of Africa, and particularly where the slave trade is carried on, with faithful men to direct that none should be brought from the coast of Africa without their own consent and the approbation of their friends, and to intercept all merchant ships that were bringing them away, until such a scrutiny was made, whatever nation they belonged to. And, I would suppose, if Great-Britain was to do any thing of this kind, that it would meet with the general approbation and assistance of other Christian nations; but whether it did or not, it could be very lawfully done at all the British forts and settlements on the coast of Africa; and particular remonstrances could be given to all the rest, to warn them of the consequences of such an evil and enormous wicked traffic as is now carried on. The Dutch have some crocodile settlers at the Cape, that should be called to a particular account for their murders and inhuman barbarities. But all the present governors of the British forts and factories should be dismissed, and faithful and good men appointed in their room; and those forts and factories, which at present are a den of thieves, might be turned into shepherd's tents, and have good shepherds sent to call the flocks to feed beside them. Then would doors of hospitality in abundance be opened in Africa to supply the weary travellers, and that immense abundance which they are enriched with, might be diffused afar; but the character of the inhabitants on the west coast of Africa, and the rich produce of their country, have been too long misrepresented by avaricious plunderers and merchants who deal in slaves; and if that country was not annually ravished and laid waste, there might be a very considerable and profitable trade carried on with the Africans. And, should the noble Britons, who have often supported their own liberties with their lives and fortunes, extend their philanthropy to abolish the slavery and oppression of the Africans, they might have settlements and many kingdoms united in a friendly alliance with themselves, which might be made greatly to their own advantage, as well as they might have the happiness of being useful to promoting the prosperity and felicity of others, who have been cruelly injured and wrongfully dealt with. Were the Africans to be dealt with in a friendly manner, and kind instruction to be administered unto them, as by degrees they became to love learning, there would be nothing in their power, but what they would wish to render their service in return for the means of improving their understanding; and the present British factories, and other settlements, might be enlarged to a very great extent. And as Great-Britain has been remarkable for ages past, for encouraging arts and sciences, and may now be put in competition with any nation in the known world, if they would take compassion on the inhabitants of the coast of Guinea, and to make use of such means as would be needful to enlighten their minds in the knowledge of Christianity, their virtue, in this respect, would have its own reward. And as the Africans became refined and established in light and knowledge, they would imitate their noble British friends, to improve their lands, and make use of that industry as the nature of their country might require, and to supply those that would trade with them, with such productions as the nature of their climate would produce; and, in every respect, the fair Britons would have the preference with them to a very great extent; and, in another respect, they would become a kind of first ornament to Great-Britain for her tender and compassionate care of such a set of distressed poor ignorant people. And were the noble Britons, and their august Sovereign, to cause protection and encouragement to be given to those Africans, they might expect in a short time, if need required it, to receive from thence great supplies of men in a lawful way, either for industry or defence; and of other things in abundance, from so great a source, where every thing is luxurious and plenty, if not laid waste by barbarity and gross ignorance. Due encouragement being given to so great, so just, and such a noble undertaking, would soon bring more revenue in a righteous way to the British nation, than ten times its share in all the profits that slavery can produce ; and such a laudable example would inspire every generous and enterprizing mind to imitate so great and worthy a nation, for establishing religion, justice, and equity to the Africans, and, in doing this, would be held in the highest esteem by all men, and be admired by all the world.

These three preceding considerations may suffice at present to shew, that some plan might be adopted in such a manner as effectually to relieve the grievances and oppression of the Africans, and to bring great honour and blessings to that nation, and to all men whosoever would endeavour to promote so great good to mankind; and it might render more conspicuous advantages to the noble Britons, as the first doers of it, and greater honour than the finding of America was at first to those that made the discovery: Though several difficulties may seem to arise at first, and the good to be sought after may appear as remote and unknown, as it was to explore the unknown regions of the Western Ocean; should it be sought after, like the intrepid Columbus, if they do not find kingdoms of wealth by the way, they may be certain of finding treasures of happiness and peace in the end. But should there be any yet alive deserving the infamy and character of all the harsh things which I have ascribed to the insidious carriers on of the slavery and commerce of the human species, they will certainly object to any thing of this kind being proposed, or ever thought of, as doing so great a good to the base Black Negroes whom they make their prey. To such I must say again, that it would be but a just commutation for what cannot be fully restored, in order to make restoration, as far as could be, for the injuries already done to them. And some may say, that if they have wages to pay to the labourers for manufacturing the West-India productions, that they would not be able to sell them at such a price as would suit the European market, unless all the different nations agreed to raise the price of their commodities in proportion. Whatever bad neighbours men may have to deal with, let the upright shew themselves to be honest men, and that difficuly, which some may fear, would be but small, as there can be no reason for men to do wrong because others do so; but as to what is consumed in Great-Britain, they could raise the price in proportion, and it would be better to sip the West-India sweetness by paying a little more money for it (if it should be found needful) than to drink the blood of iniquity at a cheaper rate. I know several ladies in England who refuse to drink sugar in their tea, because of the cruel injuries done to the Black People employed in the culture of it at the West-Indies. But should it cost the West-Indians more money to have their manufactories carried by the labour of freemen than with slaves, it would be attended with greater blessings and advantages to them in the end. What the wages should be for the labour of freemen, is a question not so easily determined; yet I should think, that it always ought to be something more than merely victuals and cloaths; and if a man works by the day, he should have the three hundredth part of what might be estimated as sufficient to keep him in necessary cloaths and provisions for a year, and, added to that, such wages of reward as their usefulness might require. Something of this kind should be observed in free countries, and then the price of provisions would be kept at such a rate as the industrious poor could live, without being oppressed and screwed down to work for nothing, but only barely to live. And were every civilized nation, where they boast of liberty, so ordered by its government, that some general and useful employment were provided for every industrious man and woman, in such a manner that none should stand still and be idle, and have to say that they could not get employment, so long as there are barren lands enough at home and abroad sufficient to employ thousands and millions of people more than there are. This, in a great measure, would prevent thieves and robbers, and the labour of many would soon enrich a nation. But those employed by the general community should only have their maintenance either given or estimated in money, and half the wages of others, which would make them seek out for something else whenever they could, and half a loaf would be better than no bread. The men that were employed in this manner, would form an useful militia, and the women would be kept from a state of misery and want, and from following a life of dissolute wickedness. Liberty and freedom, where people may starve for want, can do them but little good. We want many rules of civilization in Africa; but, in many respects, we may boast of some more essential liberties than any of the civilized nations in Europe enjoy; for the poorest amongst us are never in distress for want, unless some general and universal calamity happen to us. But if any nation or society of men were to observe the laws of God, and to keep his commandments, and walk in the way of righteousness, they would not need to fear the heat in sultry hot climates, nor the freezing inclemency of the cold, and the storms and hurricanes would not hurt them at all; they might soon see blessings and plenty in abundance showered down upon their mountains and vallies; and if his beneficence was sought after, who martials out the drops of the dew, and bids the winds to blow, and to carry the clouds on their wings to drop down their moisture and fatness on what spot soever he pleaseth, and who causeth the genial rays of the sun to warm and cherish the productions of the earth in every place according to that temperature which he sees meet; then might the temperate climes of Great-Britain be seen to vie with the rich land of Canaan of old, which is now, because of the wickedness of its inhabitants, in comparison of what it was, as only a barren desart.

Particular thanks is due to every one of that humane society of worthy and respectful gentlemen, whose liberality hath supported many of the Black poor about London. *Those that honor their Maker have mercy on the poor; and many blessings are upon the head of the just: may the fear of the Lord prolong their days, and cause their memory to be blessed, and may their number be encreased to fill their expectation with gladness*; for they have not only commiserated the poor in general, *but even those which are accounted as beasts, and imputed as vile in the sight of others.* The part that the British government has taken, to co-operate with them, has certainly a flattering and laudable appearance of doing some good; and the fitting out ships to supply a company of Black People with clothes and provisions, and to carry them to settle at Sierra Leona, in the West coast of Africa, as a free colony to Great-Britain, in a peaceable alliance with the inhabitants, has every appearance of honour, and the approbation of friends. According to the plan, humanity hath made its appearance in a more honorable way of colonization, than any Christian nation have ever done before, and may be productive of much good, if they continue to encourage and support them. But after all, there is some doubt whether their own flattering expectation in the manner as set forth to them, and the hope of their friends may not be defeated and rendered abortive; and there is some reason to fear, that they never will be settled as intended, in any permanent and peaceable way at Sierra Leona.

This prospect of settling a free colony to Great-Britain in a peaceable alliance with the inhabitants of Africa at Sierra Leona, has neither altogether met with the credulous approbation of the Africans here, nor yet been sought after with any prudent and right plan by the promoters of it. Had a treaty of agreement been first made with the inhabitants of Africa, and the terms and nature of such a settlement fixed upon, and its situation and boundary pointed out; then might the Africans, and others here, have embarked with a good prospect of enjoying happiness and prosperity themselves, and have gone with a hope of being able to render their services, in return, of some advantage to their friends and benefactors of Great-Britain. But as this was not done, and as they were to be hurried away at all events, come of them after what would; and yet, after all, to be delayed in the ships before they were set out from the coast, until many of them have perished with cold, and other disorders, and several of the most intelligent among them are dead, and others that, in all probability, would have been most useful for them were hindered from going, by means of some disagreeable jealousy of those who were appointed as governors, the great prospect of doing good seems all to be blown away. And so it appeared to some of those who are now gone, and at last, hap hazard, were obliged to go; who endeavoured in vain to get away by plunging into the water, that they might, if possible wade ashore, as dreading the prospect of their wretched fate, and as beholding their perilous situation, having every prospect of difficulty and surrounding danger.

What with the death of some of the original promoters and pro- posers of this charitable undertaking, and the death and deprivation of others that were to share the benefit of it, and by the adverse motives of those employed to be the conductors thereof, we think it will be more than what can be well expected, if we ever hear of any good in propor- tion to so great, well-designed, laudable and expensive charity. Many more of the Black People still in this country would have, with great gladness, embraced the opportunity, longing to reach their native land; but as the old saying is, A burnt child dreads the fire, some of these un- fortunate sons and daughters of Africa have been severally unlawfully dragged away from their native abodes, under various pretences, by the insidious treachery of others, and have been brought into the hands of barbarous robbers and pirates, and, like sheep to the market, have been sold into captivity and slavery, and thereby have been deprived of their natural liberty and property, and every connection that they held dear and valuable, and subjected to the cruel service of the hard-hearted brutes called planters. But some of them, by various services either to the public or to individuals, as more particularly in the course of last war, have gotten their liberty again in this free country. They are thankful for the respite, but afraid of being ensnared again; for the European seafaring people in general, who trade to foreign parts, have such a prejudice against Black People, that they use them more like asses than men, so that a Black Man is scarcely ever safe among them. Much assiduity was made use to perswade the Black People in general to embrace the opportunity of going with this company of transports; but the wiser sort declined from all thoughts of it, unless they could hear of some better plan taking place for their security and safety. For as it seemed prudent and obvious to many of them taking heed to that sacred enquiry, *Doth a fountain send forth at the same place sweet water and bitter?* They were afraid that their doom would be to drink of the bitter water. For can it be readily conceived that government would establish a free colony for them nearly on the spot, while it supports its forts and garrisons, to ensnare, merchandize, and to carry others into captivity and slavery.

Above fifty years ago, P. Gordon, in his Geography, though he was no advocate against slavery, complains of the barbarities committed against the Heathen nations, and the base usage of the negroe slaves subjected to bondage as brutes, and deprived of religion as men. His remark on the religion of the American islands, says: "As for the negroe slaves, their lot has hitherto been, and still is, to serve such Christian masters, who sufficiently declare what zeal they have for their conversion, by unkindly using a serious divine some time ago, for only proposing to endeavour the same." This was above half a century ago, and their unchristian barbarity is still continued. Even in the little time that I was in Grenada, I saw a slave receive twenty-four lashes of a whip for being seen at a church on a Sunday, instead of going to work in the fields; and those whom they put the greatest confidence in, are often served in the same manner. The noble proposals offered for instructing the heathen nations and people in his Geography, has been attended to with great supineness and indifference. The author wishes, that "sincere endeavours might be made to extend the limits of our Saviour's kingdom, with those of our own dominions; and to spread the true religion as far as the British sails have done for traffic." And he adds, "Let our planters duly consider, that to extirpate natives, is rather a supplanting than planting a new colony; and that it is far more honourable to overcome paganism in one, than to destroy a thousand pagans. Each convert is a conquest."

To put an end to the nakedness of slavery and merchandizing of men, and to prevent murder, extirpation and dissolution, is what every righteous nation ought to seek after; and to endeavour to diffuse knowledge and instruction to all the heathen nations wherever they can, is the grand duty of all Christian men. But while the horrible traffic of slavery is admitted and practiced, there can be but little hope of any good proposals meeting with success anywhere; for the abandoned carriers of it on have spread the poison of their iniquity wherever they come, at home and abroad. Were the iniquitous laws in support of it, and the whole of that oppression and injustice abolished, and the righteous laws of Christianity, equity, justice and humanity established in the room thereof, multitudes of nations would flock to the standard of truth, and instead of revolting away, they would count it their greatest happiness to be under the protection and jurisdiction of a righteous government. And in that respect, *in the multitude of the people is the King's honour; but in the want of people, is the destruction of the Prince.*

We would wish to have the grandeur and fame of the British empire to extend far and wide; and the glory and honor of God to be promoted by it, and the interest of Christianity set forth among all the nations wherever its influence and power can extend; but not to be supported by the insidious pirates, depredators, murderers and slave-holders. And as it might diffuse knowledge and instruction to others, that it might receive a tribute of reward from all its territories, forts and garrisons, without being oppressive to any. But contrary to this the wickedness of many of the White People who keep slaves, and contrary to all the laws and duties of Christianity which the Scriptures teach, they have in general endeavoured to keep the Black People in total ignorance as much as they can, which must be a great dishonor to any Christian government, and injurious to the safety and happiness of rulers.

But in order to diffuse any knowledge of Christianity to the unlearned Heathens, those who undertake to do any thing therein ought to be wise and honest men. Their own learning, though the more the better, is not so much required as that they should be men of the same mind and principles of the apostle Paul; men that would hate coveteousness, and who would hazard their lives for the cause and gospel of our Lord and Saviour Jesus Christ. "I think it needless toexpress how commendable such a design would be in itself, and how desirable the promotion thereof should be to all who stile themselves Christians, of what party or profession soever they are." Rational methods might be taken to have the Scriptures translated into many foreign languages; "and a competent number of young students of theology might be educated at home in these foreign languages, to afford a constant supply of able men, who might yearly go abroad, and be sufficiently qualified at their first arrival to undertake the great work for which they were sent." But as a hindrance to this, the many Anti-christian errors which are gone abroad into the world, and all the popish superstition and nonsense, and the various assimilations unto it, with the false philosophy which abounds among Christians, seems to threaten with an universal deluge; but God hath promised to fill the world with a knowledge of himself, and he hath set up his bow, in the rational heavens, as well as in the clouds, as a token that he will stop the proud ways of error and delusion, that hitherto they may come, and no farther. The holy arch of truth is to be seen in the azure paths of the pious and wise, and conspicuously painted in crimson over the martyrs tombs. These, with the golden altars of truth, built up by the reformed churches, and many pious, good and righteous men, are bulwarks that will ever stand against all the forts of error. Teaching would be exceeding necessary to the pagan nations and ignorant people in every place and situation; but they do not need any unscriptural forms and ceremonies to be taught unto them; they can devise superstitions enough among themselves, and church government too, if ever they need any.

And hence we would agree in this one thing with that erroneous philosopher, who has lately wrote *An Apology for Negro Slavery*, "But if the slave is only to be made acquainted with the form, without the substance; if he is only to be decked out with the external trappings of religion; if he is only to be taught the uncheering principles of gloomy superstition; or, if he is only to be inspired with the intemperate frenzy of enthusiastic fanaticism, it were better that he remained in that dark state, where he could not see good from ill." But these words *intemperate, frenzy, enthusiastic, and fanaticism* may be variously applied, and often wrongfully; but, perhaps never better, or more fitly, than to be ascribed as the genuine character of this author's brutish philosophy; and he may subscribe it, and the meaning of these words, with as much affinity to himself, as he bears a relation to a *Hume*, or to his friend *Tobin*. The poor negroes in the West-Indies, have suffered enough by such religion as the philosophers of the North produce; Protestants, as they are called, are the most barbarous slave-holders, and there are none can equal the Scotch floggers and negroe-drivers, and the barbarous Dutch cruelties. Perhaps as the church of Rome begins to sink in its power, its followers may encrease in virtue and humanity; so that many, who are the professed adherents thereof, would even blush and abhor the very mention of the cruelty and bloody deeds that their ancestors have committed; and we find slavery itself more tolerable among them, than it is in the Protestant countries.

But I shall add another observation, which I am sorry to find among Christians, and I think it is a great deficiency among the clergy in general, when covetous and profligate men are admitted amongst them, who either do not know, or dare not speak the truth, but neglect their duty much, or do it with such supineness, that it becomes good for nothing. Sometimes an old woman selling matches, will preach a better, and a more orthodox sermon, than some of the clergy, who are only decked out (as Mr. Turnbul calls it) with the external trappings of religion. Much of the great wickedness of others lieth at their door, and these words of the Prophet are applicable to them: *And first, saith the Lord, I will recompence their iniquity, and their sin double; because they have defiled my land, they have filled mine inheritance with the carcases of their detestable and abominable things.* Such are the errors of men. Church, signifies an assembly of people; but a building of wood, brick or stone, where the people meet together, is generally called so; and should the people be frightened away by the many abominable dead carcases which they meet with, they should follow the multitudes to the fields, to the vallies, to the mountains, to the islands, to the rivers, and to the ships, and compel them to come in, that the house of the Lord may be filled. But when we find some of the covetous connivers with slave-holders, in the West-Indies, so ignorant as to dispute whether a Pagan can be baptized without giving him a Christian name, we cannot expect much from them, or think that they will follow after much good. No name, whether Christian or Pagan, has any thing to do with baptism; if the requisite qualities of knowledge and faith be found in a man, he may be baptized let his name be what it will. And Christianity does not require that we should be deprived of our own personal name, or the name of our ancestors; but it may very fitly add another name unto us, Christian, or one anointed. And it might as well be answered so to that question in the English liturgy, *What is your name?*—A Christian.

> "A Christian is the highest stile of man!
> And is there, who the blessed cross wipes off
> As a foul blot, from his dishonor'd brow?
> If angels tremble, 'tis at such a sight:
> The wretch they quit disponding of their charge,
> More struck with grief or wonder who can tell?"

And let me now hope that you will pardon me in all that I have been thus telling you, O ye inhabitants of Great-Britain! to whom I owe the greatest respect; to your king! to yourselves! and to your government! And tho' many things which I have written may seem harsh, it cannot be otherwise evaded when such horible iniquity is transacted: and tho' to some what I have said may appear as the rattling leaves of autumn, that may soon be blown away and whirled in a vortex where few can hear and know: I must yet say, although it is not for me to determine the manner, that the voice of our complaint implies a vengeance, because of the great iniquity that you have done, and because of the cruel injustice done unto us Africans; and it ought to sound in your ears as the rolling waves around your circum-ambient shores; and if it is not hearkened unto, it may yet arise with a louder voice, as the rolling thunder, and it may encrease in the force of its volubility, not only to shake the leaves of the most stout in heart, but to rend the mountains before them, and to cleave in pieces the rocks under them, and to go on with fury to smite the stoutest oaks in the forest; and even to make that which is strong, and wherein you think that your strength lieth, to become as stubble, and as the fibres of rotten wood, that will do you no good, and your trust in it will become a snare of infatuation to you!

FINIS.

Poetry

THE NEGRO'S COMPLAINT

Forced from home and all its pleasures,
  Afric's coast I left forlorn;
To increase a stranger's treasures,
  O'er the raging billows borne.
Men from England bought and sold me,
  Paid my price in paltry gold;
But, though slave they have enrolled me,
  Minds are never to be sold.

Still in thought as free as ever,
  What are England's rights, I ask,
Me from my delights to sever,
  Me to torture, me to task?
Fleecy locks and black complexion
  Cannot forfeit nature's claim;
Skins may differ, but affection
  Dwells in white and black the same.

Why did all-creating nature
  Make the plant for which we toil?
Sighs must fan it, tears must water,
  Sweat of ours must dress the soil.
Think, ye masters iron-hearted,
  Lolling at your jovial boards,
Think how many backs have smarted
  For the sweets your cane affords.

Is there, as ye sometimes tell us,
  Is there One who reigns on high?
Has He bid you buy and sell us,
  Speaking from his throne, the sky?
Ask him, if your knotted scourges,

Matches, blood-extorting screws,
Are the means that duty urges
   Agents of his will to use?

Hark! He answers!--Wild tornadoes
   Strewing yonder sea with wrecks,
Wasting towns, plantations, meadows,
   Are the voice with which he speaks.
He, foreseeing what vexations
   Afric's sons should undergo,
Fixed their tyrants' habitations
   Where his whirlwinds answer- No.

By our blood in Afric wasted
   Ere our necks received the chain;
By the miseries that we tasted,
   Crossing in your barks the main;
By our sufferings, since ye brought us
   To the man-degrading mart.
All sustained by patience, taught us
   Only by a broken heart!

Deem our nation brutes no longer,
   Till some reason ye shall find
Worthier of regard and stronger
   Than the colour of our kind.
Slaves of gold, whose sordid dealings
   Tarnish all your boasted powers,
Prove that you have human feelings
   Ere you proudly question ours!

PITY FOR POOR AFRICANS

Video meliora proboque,
Deteriora sequor.

I own I am shock'd at the purchase of slaves,
And fear those who buy them and sell them are knaves;
What I hear of their hardships, their tortures, and groans
Is almost enough to draw pity from stones.

I pity them greatly, but I must be mum,
For how could we do without sugar and rum?
Especially sugar, so needful we see?
What? give up our desserts, our coffee, and tea!

Besides, if we do, the French, Dutch, and Danes,
Will heartily thank us, no doubt, for our pains;
If we do not buy the poor creatures, they will,
And tortures and groans will be multiplied still.

If foreigners likewise would give up the trade,
Much more in behalf of your wish might be said;
But while they get riches by purchasing blacks,
Pray tell me why we may not also go snacks?

Your scruples and arguments bring to my mind
A story so pat, you may think it is coin'd,
On purpose to answer you, out of my mint;
But, I can assure you, I saw it in print.

A youngster at school, more sedate than the rest,
Had once his integrity put to the test;
His comrades had plotted an orchard to rob,
And ask'd him to go and assist in the job.

He was. shock'd,sir, like you, and answer'd -- Oh,no
What! rob our good neighbour! I pray you, don't go;
Besides, the the man's poor, his orchard's his bread,
Then think of his children, for they must be fed."

150

"You speak very fine, and you look very grave,
But apples we want, and apples we'll have;
If you will go with us, you shall have a share,
If not, you shall have neither apple nor pear."

They spoke, and Tom ponder'd -- !I see they will gc:
Poor man! what a pity to injuro him so
Poor man! I would save him his fruit if I could,
But staying behind will do him no good.

"If the matter depended alone upon me,
His apples might hang till they dropt from the tree;
But, since they will take them, I think I'll go too,
He will lose none by me, though I get a few."

His scruples thus silenc'd, Tom felt more at ease,
And went with his comrades the apples to seize;
He blam'd and protested, but join'd in the plan;
He shar'd in the plunder, but pitied the man.

THE MORNING DREAM

Twas in the glad season of spring,
  Asleep at the dawn of the day,
I dream'd what I cannot but sing,
  So pleasant it seem'd as I lay.
I dream'd, that on ocean afloat,
  Far hence to the westward I sail'd,
While the billows high lifted the boat,
  And the fresh-blowing breeze never fail'd.

In the steerage a woman I saw,
  Such, at least, was the form that she wore,
Whose beauty impress'd me with awe
  Ne'er taught me by woman before.
She sat, and a shield at her side
  Shed light, like a Sun on the waves,
And, smiling divinely, she cried-
  "I go to make freemen of slaves."

Then raising her voice to a strain
  The sweetest that ear ever heard,
She sung of the slave's broken chain,
  Wherever her glory appear'd.
Some clouds, which had over us hung,
  Fled chased by her melody clear,
And, methought while she Liberty sung,
  'Twas liberty only to hear.

Thus, swiftly dividing the flood,
  To a slave-cultur'd island we came,
Where a demon, her enemy, stood-
  Oppression his terrible name.
In his hand, as a sign of his sway,
  A scourge hung with lashes he bore,
And stood looking out for his prey
  From Africa's sorrowful shore.

But soon as approaching the land
  That Goddess-like woman he view'd,
The scourge he let fall from his hand,
  With blood of his subjects imbrued.
I saw him both sicken and die,
  And, the moment the monster expired,
Heard shouts which ascended the sky,
  From thousands with rapture inspired.

Awakening, how could I but muse
  At what such a dream should betide?
But soon my ear caught the glad news
  Which served my weak thought for a gu̶de,-
That Britannia, renown'd o'er the waves,
  For the hatred she ever has shown
To the black-sceptred rulers of slaves,
  Resolves to have none of her own.

SWEET MEAT HAS SOUR SAUCE;
OR, THE SLAVE-TRADER IN THE DUMPS.

A TRADER I am to the African shore,
But since that my trading is like to be o'er,
I'll sing you a song that you ne'er heard before,
      Which nobody can deny, deny,
      Which nobody can deny.

When I first heard the news it gave me a shock,
Much like what they call an electrical knock,
And now I am going to sell off my stock,
      Which nobody, &c.

'Tis a curious assortment of dainty regales,
To tickle the negroes with when the ship sails,
Fine chains for the neck, and a cat with nine tails,
      Which nobody, &c.

Here's supple-jack plenty, and store of ratan,
That will wind itself round the sides of a man,
As close as a hoop round a bucket or can,
      Which nobody, &c.

Here's padlocks and bolts, and screws for the thumbs,
That squeeze them so lovingly till the blood comes,
They sweeten the temper like comforts or plums,
      Which nobody, &c.

When a negro his head from his victuals withdraws,
And clenches his teeth and thrusts out his paws,
Here's a notable engine to open his jaws,
      Which nobody, &c.

Thus going to market, we kindly prepare
A pretty black cargo of African ware,
For what they must meet with when they get there,
      Which nobody, &c.

'Twould do your heart good to see 'em below,
Lie flat on their backs all the way as we go,
Like sprats on a gridiron, scores in a row,
   Which nobody, &c.

But ah! if in vain I have studied an art
So gainful to me, all boasting apart,
I think it will break my compassionate heart,
   Which nobody, &c.

For oh! how it enters my soul like an awl;
This pity, which some people self-pity call,
Is sure the most heart-piercing pity of all,
   Which nobody, &c.

So this is my song, as I told you before;
Come, buy off my stock, for I must no more
Carry Caesars and Pompeys to sugar-cane shore,
   Which nobody &c.

Poems Concerning the Slave Trade
Robert Southey

Sonnet I

Hold your mad hands! for ever on your plain
Must the gorged vulture clog his beak with blood?
For ever must your Niger's tainted flood
Roll to the ravenous shark his banquet slain?
Hold your mad hands! And learn at length to know,
And turn your vengeance on the common foe,
Yon treacherous vessel and her godless crew!
Let never traders with false pretext fair
Set on your shores again their wicked feet:
With interdict and indignation meet
Repel them, and with fire and sword pursue!
Avarice, the white, cadaverous fiend, is there,
Who spreads his toils accursed wide and far,
And for his purveyor calls the demon War.

Sonnet II

Why dost thou beat thy breast and rend thine hair,
And to the deaf sea pour thy frantic cries?
Before the gale the laden vessel flies;
The Heavens all-favoring smile, the breeze is fair;
Hark to the clamors of the exulting crew!
Hark, how their cannon mock the patient skies!
Why dost thou shriek, and strain thy red-swollen eyes,
As the white sail is lessening from thy view?
Go, pine in want, and anguish, and despair;
There is no mercy found in human-kind;
Go, Widow, to thy grave, and rest thee there!
But may the God of Justice bid the wind
Whelm that curst bark beneath the mountain wave,
And bless with Liberty and Death the Slave!

Sonnet III

Oh, he is worn with toil! the big drops run
Down his dark cheek; hold--hold thy merciless hand,
Pale tyrant! for beneath thy hard command
O'erwearied nature sinks. The scorching sun,
As pitiless as proud Prosperity,
Darts on him his full beams; gasping he lies
Arraigning with his looks the patient skies,
While that inhuman trader lifts on high
The mangling scourge. O ye who at your ease
Sip the blood-sweeten'd beverage, thoughts like these
Haply ye scorn: I thank thee, Gracious God!
That I do feel upon my cheek the glow
Of indignation, when beneath the rod
A sable brother writhes in silent woe.

Sonnet IV

'Tis night; the unrelenting owners sleep
As undisturb'd as Justice; but no more
The o'erwearied Slave, as on his native shore,
Rests on his reedy couch: he wakes to weep!
Though through the toil and anguish of the day
No tear escaped him, not one suffering groan
Beneath the twisted thong, he weeps alone
In bitterness; thinking that far away
While happy Negroes join the midnight song,
And merriment resounds on Niger's shore,
She whom he loves, far from the cheerful throng
Stands sad, and gazes from her lowly door
With dim-grown eye, silent and woe-begone,
And weeps for him who will return no more.

Sonnet V

Did then the Negro rear at last the Sword
Of vengeance? Did he plunge its thirsty blade
In the cold heart of his inhuman lord?
Oh, who shall blame him? in the midnight shade
There came on him the intolerable thought
Of every past delight; his native grove,
Friendship's best joys, and liberty and love,
Forever lost! Such recollections wrought
His brain to madness. Wherefore should he live
Longer with abject patience to endure
His wrongs and wretchedness, when hope can give
No consolation, time can bring no cure?
But justice for himself he yet could take,
And life is then well given for vengence' sake.

Sonnet VI

High in the air exposed the slave is hung,
To all the birds of Heaven, their living food!
He groans not, though awaked by that fierce sun
New torturers live to drink their parent blood:
He groans not, though the gorging vulture tear
The quivering fibre. Hither look, O ye
Who tore this man from peace and liberty!
Look hither, ye who weigh with polotic care
The gain against the guilt! Beyond the grave
There is another world! – bear ye in mind,
Ere your decree proclaims to all mankind
The gain is worth the guilt, that there the Slave,
Before the Eternal, "thunder-tongued shall plead
Against the deep damnation of your deed."

To the Genius of Africa

O thou, who from the mountain's height
Rollest thy clouds with all their weight
Of waters to old Nile's majestic tide;
Or o'er the dark, sepulchral plain
Recallest Carthage in her ancient pride,
The Mistress of the Main;
Hear, Genius, hear thy children's cry!
Not always shouldst thou love to brood
Stern o'er the desert solitude
Where seas of sand heave their hot surges high;
Nor, genius, should the midnight song
Detain thee in some milder mood
The palmy plains among,
Where Gambia to the torches' light
Flows radiant through the awaken'd night.

   Ah, linger not to hear the song!
Genius, avenge thy children's wrong!
The demon Avarice on your shore
Brings all the horrors of his train;
And hark! where from the field of gore
Howls the hyena o'er the slain!
Lo! where the flaming village fires the skies,
Avenging Power awake! arise!

   Arise thy children's wrong redress!
Heed the mother's wretchedness,
When in the hot, infectious air
O'er her sick babe she bows opprest, --
Hear her when the Traders tear
The suffering infant from her breast!
Sunk in the ocean he shall rest!
Hear thou the wretched mother's cries,
Avenging Power! awake! arise!

By the rank, infected air
That taints those cabins of despair;
By the scourges blacken'd o'er,
And stiff and hard with human gore
By every groan of deep distress,
By every curse of wretchedness;
The vices and the crimes that flow
From the hopelessness of woe;
By every drop of blood bespilt,
By Afric's wrongs and Europe's guilt,
Awake! arise! avenge!

And thou hast heard! and o'er their blood-fed plains
Swept thine avenging hurricanes;
And bade thy storms with whirlwind roar
Dash their proud navies on the shore;
And where their armies claim d the fight
Wither'd the warrior's might;
And o'er the unholy host with baneful breath,
There, Genius, thou hast breathed the gales of Death.

THE SAILOR,

WHO HAD SERVED IN THE SLAVE TRADE

In September, 1798, a Dissenting Minister of Bristol discovered a sailor in the neighborhood of that City, groaning and praying in a cow-house. The circumstances which occasioned his agony of mind detailed in the annexed ballad, without the slightest addition or alteration. By presenting it as a Poem, the story is made more public; and such stories ought to be made as public as possible.

It was a Christian minister,
  Who, in the month of flowers,
Walk'd forth at eve amid the fields
  Near Bristol's ancient towers, –

When, form a lonely out-house breathed,
  He heard a voice of woe,
And groans which less might seem from pain,
  Than wretchedness, to flow.

Heart-rending groans they were, with words
  Of bitterest despair;
Yet with the holy name of Christ
  Pronounced in broken prayer.

The Christian Minister went in;
  A Sailor there he sees,
Whose hands were lifted up to Heaven,
  And he was on his knees.

Nor did the sailor, so intent,
  His entering footsteps heed,
But now "Our Father" said, and now
  His half-forgotten creed; –

And often on our Savior call'd
  With many a bitter groan,
But in such anguish as may spring
  From deepest guilt alone.

The miserable man was ask'd
   Why he was kneeling there,
And what had been the crime that caused
   The anguish of his prayer.

"I have done a cursed thing!" he cried;
   "It haunts me night and day;
And I have sought this lonely place
   Here undisturb'd to pray.

Aboard I have no place for prayer,
   So I came here alone,
That I might freely kneel and pray,
   And call on Christ, and groan.

If to the main-mast head I go,
   The Wicked One is there;
From place to place, from rope to rope,
   He follows me everywhere.

I shut my eyes – it matters not –
   Still, still the same I see,–
And when I lie me down at night,
   'Tis always day with me!

He follows, follows every where,
   And every place is Hell!
O God – and I must go with Him
   In endless fire to dwell?

He follows, follows every where;
   He's still above – below!
Oh, tell me where to fly from him
   Oh, tell me where to go!"

"But tell thou" quoth the stranger then,
   "What this thy crime hath been;
So haply I may comfort give
   To one who grieves for sin."

"Oh cursed, cursed is the deed!"
　　The wretched man replies;
"And night, and day, and every where,
　　'Tis still before my eyes.

I sail'd on board a Guinea-man,
　　And to the slave-coast went; –
Would that the sea had swallow'd me
　　When I was innocent!

And we took in our cargo there,
　　Three hundred negro slaves,
And we sail'd homeward merrily
　　Over the ocean-waves.

But some were sulky of the slaves,
　　And would not touch their meat,
So therefore we were forced by threats
　　And blows to make them eat.

One woman, sulkier than the rest,
　　Would still refuse her food, –
O Jesus God! I hear her cries!
　　I see her in her blood!

The Captain made me tie her up,
　　And flog while he stood by;
And then he cursed me if I stayed
　　My hand to hear her cry.

She shriek'd, she groan'd, – I could not spare,
　　For the Captain he stood by; –
Dear God! that I might rest one night
　　From that poor creature's cry!

What woman's child a sight like that
　　Could bear to look upon!
And still the Captain would not spare –
　　But made me still flog on.

She could not be more glad than I,
    When she was taken down:
A blessed minute! – 't was the last
    That I have ever known

I did not close my eyes all night,
    Thinking what I had done;
I heard her groans, and they grew faint
    Towards the rising sun.

She groan'd and moan'd , but her voice grew
    Fainter at morning tide;
Fainter and fainter until it came,
    Until at noon she died.

They flung her overboard; – poor wretch,
    She rested from her pain, –
But when – O Christ! O blessed God! –
    Shall I have rest again?

I saw the sea close over her;
    Yet she is still in sight;
I see her twisting every where;
    I hear her day and night.

Go where I will, do what I can,
    The Wicked One I see:
Dear Christ, have mercy on my soul!
    O God, deliver me!

Oh, give me comfort, if you can!
    Oh, tell me where to fly!
Oh, tell me if there can be hope
    For one so lost as I!"

What said the Minister of Christ?
    He bade him trust in Heaven,
And call on Him for whose dear sake
    All sins shall be forgiven.

He told him of that precious blood
   Which should his guilt efface;
Told him that none are lost, but they
   Who turn from proffer'd grace.

He bade him pray, and knelt with him,
   And join'd him in his prayers: –
And some who read this dreadful tale
   Perhaps will aid with theirs.

Suggested Reading

The Transatlantic Slave Trade

Eltis, David. *Economic Growth and the Ending of the Transatlantic Slave Trade*. New York: Oxford UP, 1987.

Klingberg, Frank J. *The Anti-Slavery Movement in England: A Study in English Humanitarianism*. Archon Books, 1968.

Kowaleski-Wallace, Elizabeth. *The British Slave Trade and Public Memory*. New York: Columbia UP, 2006.

Rawley, James A., and Stephen D. Behrendt. *The Transatlantic Slave Trade : A History*. Lincoln: University of Nebraska Press, 2005.

Richardson, David, Suzanne Schwarz, and Anthony Tibbles, eds. *Liverpool and Transatlantic Slavery*. Liverpool: Liverpool UP, 2007.

Thomas, Hugh. *The Slave Trade: the Story of the Atlantic Slave Trade, 1440-1870*. New York: Simon & Schuster, 1997.

Fighting Against the Transatlantic Slave Trade

Diouf, Silviane A., ed. *Fighting the Slave Trade: West African Strategies*. Athens: Ohio UP, 2003.

Sharp, Granville. *Extract from a Representation of the Injustice and Dangerous Tendency of Tolerating Slavery, or Admitting the Least Claim of Private Property in the Persons of Men in England*. London, 1769.

Wahab, Amar, and Cecily Jones, eds. *Free at Last? Reflections on Freedom and the Abolition of the British Transatlantic Slave Trade*. Newcastle upon Tyne: Cambridge Scholars, 2011.

Wilberforce, William. *A Practical View of the Prevailing Religious System of Professed Christians, in the Higher and Middle Classes in This Country, Contrasted with Real Christianity*. Sixth ed. London, 1798.

Wilberforce, William. *An Appeal to the Religion, Justice, and Humanity of the Inhabitants of the British Empire, in Behalf of the Negro Slaves in the West Indies*. London, 1823.

Support for the Human Trafficking of Africans

Doubts on the Abolition of the Slave Trade. London, 1790.

Ramsey, James. *Objections to the Abolition of the Slave Trade, with Answers*. Second ed. London, 1788.

Schwarz, Suzanne, ed. *The Career of James Irving in the Liverpool Slave Trade*. Liverpool: Liverpool UP, 1995.

Literature on the Slave Trade

Bailey, Anne C. *African Voices of the Atlantic Slave Trade*. Boston: Beacon, 2005.

Equiano, Olaudah. *The Interesting Narrative of the Life of Olaudah Equiano, or Gustavus Vassa, the African*. 1789.

Lovejoy, Paul E. "'Freedom Narratives' of Transatlantic Slavery." *Slavery & Abolition: A Journal of Slave and Post-Slave Studie* 32.1 (2011): 91-107. *Taylor & Francis Online*.

Thomas, Helen. *Romanticism and Slave Narratives: Transatlantic Testimonies*. Port Melbourne: Cambridge UP, 2003.

Lasting Effects of the Slave Trade on Africa

Burnett, Patrick, and Firoze Manji, eds. *From the Slave Trade to 'Free' Trade: How Trade Undermines Democracy and Justice in Africa.* Cape Town: Pambazuka, 2011.

Murphy, Laura T. *Metaphor and the Slave Trade in West African Literature.* Athens: Ohio UP, 2012.

www.ingramcontent.com/pod-product-compliance
Lightning Source LLC
Chambersburg PA
CBHW032106280326
41933CB00009B/768